IT'S NOT TOO LATE

THE ESSENTIAL PART YOU PLAY IN SHAPING YOUR TEEN'S FAITH

DAN DUPEE

BakerBooks
a division of Baker Publishing Group
Grand Rapids, Michigan

© 2016 by Dan Dupee

Published by Baker Books
a division of Baker Publishing Group
P.O. Box 6287, Grand Rapids, MI 49516-6287
www.bakerbooks.com

Printed in the United States of America

Library of Congress Cataloging-in-Publication Data
Names: Dupee, Dan, author.
Title: It's not too late : the essential part you play in shaping your teen's faith / Dan Dupee.
Description: Grand Rapids, MI : Baker Books, 2016. | Includes bibliographical references. | Description based on print version record and CIP data provided by publisher; resource not viewed.
Identifiers: LCCN 2015041467 (print) | LCCN 2015040655 (ebook) | ISBN 9781493401628 (ebook) | ISBN 9780801018602 (pbk.)
Subjects: LCSH: Christian education of teenagers. | Parent and teenager. | Parenting—Religious aspects—Christianity.
Classification: LCC BV1485 (print) | LCC BV1485 .D87 2016 (ebook) | DDC 248.8/45—dc23
LC record available at http://lccn.loc.gov/2015041467

Unless otherwise indicated, Scripture quotations are from the Holy Bible, New International Version®. NIV®. Copyright © 1973, 1978, 1984, 2011 by Biblica, Inc.™ Used by permission of Zondervan. All rights reserved worldwide. www.zondervan.com

Scripture quotations labeled ESV are from The Holy Bible, English Standard Version® (ESV®), copyright © 2001 by Crossway, a publishing ministry of Good News Publishers. Used by permission. All rights reserved. ESV Text Edition: 2007

Scripture quotations labeled GNT are from the Good News Translation—Second Edition. Copyright © 1992 by American Bible Society. Used by permission.

Scripture quotations labeled KJV are from the King James Version of the Bible.

Scripture quotations labeled Message are from The Message by Eugene H. Peterson, copyright © 1993, 1994, 1995, 2000, 2001, 2002. Used by permission of NavPress Publishing Group. All rights reserved.

Scripture quotations labeled NLT are from the Holy Bible, New Living Translation, copyright © 1996, 2004, 2007 by Tyndale House Foundation. Used by permission of Tyndale House Publishers, Inc., Carol Stream, Illinois 60188. All rights reserved.

Some names and details have been changed to protect the privacy of the individuals involved.

16   17   18   19   20   21   22   7   6   5   4   3   2   1

"Parenting is the most difficult, painful, glorious and sweet gift I have known in this life. Parenting college-aged young adults is as complex as any calling on earth. Dan Dupee—a parent, an educator, and president of one of the most remarkable college ministries in America—offers tender, humbly wise, and compelling counsel for walking the tightrope of parenting children who are of the age to not want to be parented. Dan guides us to neither give in to the need to micromanage or justify cowardly detachment. Further, he explores the wealth of opportunities to participate in learning to join your child in the adventure of making faith the framework to explore all knowledge. Your relationship with your child will grow far beyond your wildest dreams as you explore this glorious book."

Dan B. Allender, professor of counseling psychology and founding president of The Seattle School of Theology and Psychology; author of *How Children Raise Parents* and *Healing the Wounded Heart*

"Dan Dupee has great news for all of us raising teenagers: We continue to be the most influential people in our kids' lives. With biblical wisdom and a healthy dose of common sense, Dan encourages us to realize that our teenagers need us now more than ever—and with love and guidance, we can send our kids out into the world with a vibrant faith of their own."

Jim Daly, president of Focus on the Family

"As a parent of two teenagers, I found *It's Not Too Late* both encouraging and empowering. Dan Dupee deconstructs myths that leave moms and dads feeling inadequate to influence their children's faith and replaces them with God's wisdom, grounded in Scripture, sociological research, and anecdotal experience. You will find help and hope in these pages!"

Jerusha Clark, coauthor of *Your Teenager's Not Crazy*

"*It's Not Too Late*. That is Dan Dupee's important message to parents of children who are in the transition from child to adult. As a college professor myself, I see many people in this age group every day, and while they are coming under other influences, I agree that parents remain vitally important in the lives of these young men and women. Dan gives great practical advice based on theological insight and, out of his long experience as CEO of the Coalition for Christian Outreach, a deep knowledge of this age group and their parents. Every parent ought to read this book!"

Tremper Longman III, Robert H. Gundry Professor
of Biblical Studies, Westmont College

"There is no one I trust more on this topic of raising kids who can transition well into their young adult and college years than Dan Dupee. I've watched his leadership within the campus ministry organization he leads and how he pays attention to the ways young adults thrive and grow, and I've seen his family, including his own young adult kids, and admire them greatly. This book is one of a kind, bringing together great stories with reliable research, helpful biblical truth, and keen insight gleaned from focus groups and interviews with parents of older teens and young adults. He knows the issues and he has learned what works, even in difficult times and in painfully messy situations. Our culture implies that parents have little influence over their college-aged sons and daughters, but Dupee proves otherwise and invites us to hopeful, engaged, positive parenting. This book will be reassuring and helpful to parents and will change the tone of the conversation about emerging adults in the church."

Byron Borger, Hearts & Minds Books

To my wife, Carol,
truly a woman of noble character,
and to our parents,
Dave and Kay Dupee and Jerry and Mary Gail Korsmeyer,
who have shown us how
to love our kids by loving us.

Contents

Contents

Introduction

There's Hope for Your Great, Scary Expectations

You're in a classroom with an unlikely collection of people (the guy behind the meat counter at the grocery store next to your college sweetheart), while someone who looks vaguely like a professor begins to pass out a final exam. The feeling in your stomach goes from butterflies to pre-ulcer panic, because—son of a gun!—you forgot to show up at this class for an entire semester! You realize this is not going to turn out well at all. To make the whole experience complete, you are not wearing pants.

Thankfully, at this point you begin to wake up and shake off the dream. *Hey, wait a minute,* you think. *I haven't taken a final exam in thirty years, and I've never been in a classroom with the guy behind the meat counter.* Whew! Your subconscious has been working overtime on some loose end in your life—something capable of producing regular anxiety.

If you are a Christian parent of a child ranging from sixteen to twenty-three, I have at least one idea of what might be making you

9

anxious. You might be turning two questions around repeatedly in your head: "Will my child navigate the dangers of post-high school and make a successful transition into adulthood? When my child gets to the other side of college or into the job market, will he or she still be following Christ?"

At the core of your anxiety is your changing relationship with your child. While your child is navigating his or her most turbulent, life-defining season, you feel ill-equipped to help. Worse yet, you feel your own sense of power to guide your child shrinking at an accelerated rate. In fact, according to popular culture, your time of influence is past, and your child's peers are far more important than you are.

You might even think of yourself as in a dead zone. When your child was a toddler, you had some control; when he or she was in elementary school, you were perceived to know everything. Now that your child is sixteen to twenty-three, you know nothing and are relegated to the role of observer, financier, and prayer warrior. Your child might eventually come to value your opinion again, but by then it may be too late. For now, you're in an anxiety-inducing dead zone. You may fear your best efforts haven't been enough or your failures have far overshadowed your successes. In many cases, you have to watch your child in transition from a geographical distance as the behavior boundaries of a kid living at home are dissolved.

As a Christian parent of four young adults, two newly post-college and two in college, I'm familiar with the anxiety. To me, nothing is more important than my kids having and living out a vibrant relationship with Christ. Of course, I also want them to grow into mature, healthy, and independent adults.

In addition to being a parent of four, I am former president and now chairman of the board of the Coalition for Christian Outreach (CCO), a campus ministry. Over the past seventeen years, I've shared coffee or meals with countless parents struggling with a sense of powerlessness as their children navigate the most turbulent years of life. Christian parents in this state look to youth pastors, youth trips, and campus ministry to do what they feel they can't do: influence their child in healthy spiritual and life-affirming ways. Christian parents look to people like me for answers.

Over the years, I've worked hard to uncover every answer I could find. I've searched biblical and sociological materials, some of which I'll describe in this introduction. I was unable, however, to find satisfying sources that address the role of Christian parents in the lives of their adolescent children. As a parent, and as one who serves struggling parents as his life's work, I looked for a practical guide to navigate these troubled waters. It's not that I expected a simple, straightforward formula with direct cause-and-effect results. People are messy, and parenting is messy. Even so, there had to be principles and practical guidelines to follow. God would not leave us powerless in the lives of the very children he gave us.

It was time to go to a source plentifully available to the CCO: Christian parents. Although the CCO ministry is to students, parents and concerned adults finance our work. Our reach extends to the most concerned parents (willing to spend cash to support college ministry) across a wide spectrum. The CCO works annually with over 32,000 college students on 115 campuses spread across 8 states in the Mid-Atlantic and part of the Midwest. We have 251 staff and over 67 formal partnerships with churches, colleges, and community organizations and a number of informal connections. We are connected to a lot of parents.

I decided to host a series of focus groups composed of parents, the vast majority of whom are raising adolescents, and young adults. I sought to learn about parenting from parents: what is working, what isn't, and what their adult children are saying has been spiritually valuable. Where do parents judge themselves successful and where do they perceive failure? What are their deepest anxieties and what are they doing to address those anxieties? Most important, what principles, biblical and otherwise, can we glean to help those parents next in line?

My goal was to combine what I could learn from parent focus groups with what we know from Scripture and other reputable sources to create positive pathways for parents. I didn't expect these pathways to make parenting black-and-white but sought to guide parents in the context of their search for wisdom regarding each individual child. While my goal was to be practical, it wasn't to pretend that a cause-and-effect equation is all we need to guide emerging adults. My goal was to help parents build constructive pathways where they could confidently walk with their emerging adults.

In Scripture, God never directly addresses the question, "How do I get my sixteen-year-old to engage in conversation at the dinner table (or at least use polysyllabic words)?" Jesus didn't tell a parable on the issue of kids home from college and curfews. Even so, the Bible is overflowing with wisdom for parents, much of it fitting for the emerging adult transition. I did my best to dig into biblical teachings about parenting, influence, and wisdom.

While I was digging into Scripture and other sources, I held the focus groups. Sixty-seven parents participated in nine different group interview sessions over a five-month period. The results were amazing. The focus groups revealed information I might expect, but they also revealed surprises that revolutionized my thinking. For example, I learned that although parents relentlessly seek to shield their children from suffering, difficulties and trials can be experiences that positively shape a child's faith. These struggles can create opportunities for a child to connect with God in a personally relevant way.

When it comes to sociological research, the starting point was a survey done by the Barna Group and subsequent writing and speaking done by Barna's president, David Kinnaman. I particularly turned to the book *UnChristian*, which Kinnaman coauthored with Gabe Lyons. My primary sociological research source was the National Study of Youth and Religion (NSYR), as presented in the book *Souls in Transition* by Christian Smith with Patricia

Snell, and again in Kenda Creasy Dean's *Almost Christian: What the Faith of Our Teenagers Is Telling the American Church*. Sociologist Vern Bengston's recent book *Families and Faith: How Religion Is Passed Down across Generations* (with Norella M. Putney and Susan Harris) became an important secondary source, particularly on the role of fathers.

I also drew on two very good books on the college transition: *Make College Count* by Derek Melleby and *Sticky Faith* by Dr. Kara E. Powell and Dr. Chap Clark. The best book on the next big transition, from college to the real world, is Steven Garber's *The Fabric of Faithfulness*, which I read with this project in mind.

From the synergy of these sources, I learned one resounding truth: the whole idea of a dead zone of parental influence is off the mark, perpetuated by a number of myths that even Christian parents typically fail to question. It turns out that Christian parents have more influence on their kids than anyone else does.

This book puts forth good news and a call to action: *Christian parents can and must reclaim a healthy place of influence in the lives of their young adult children.* If you are a parent of an emerging adult, you'll find encouragement and help in these pages. If you are a less-than-perfect parent (as we all are), if you do your parenting in less-than-ideal circumstances, or if you feel you are stumbling blindly along, it's okay. You still have the opportunity to influence your child positively for Christ under an umbrella of grace.

It's not too late.

1

A Foundation of Wisdom

Is there anything you've undertaken—any goal, challenge, or project—that has been harder or more rewarding than raising a child? There is no easy formula for parenting, and here is at least part of the reason why: being human is messy, and parenting emerging human adults is messy. As I facilitated parent focus groups, I encountered surprising lessons within some messy stories. An exchange from a focus group in Philadelphia is a good example.

On one end of the table sat the parents of five kids, each child managing the transition from high school, to college, to young adulthood quite well. Tom and Alice's kids all "own their faith" as Christian young people, practice Christian disciplines, are members of churches, and make good decisions.

Also at the table sat Mike and Michele, parents whose son and daughter were on a different path. Two years ago, Mike and Michele's daughter moved in with her boyfriend. Last year, just as their son was preparing to leave for a semester abroad, his girlfriend became pregnant.

Now Mike and Michele, who are wonderful Christian people, are grandparents. Both of their children have made choices that will permanently affect their futures: their daughter has no desire to follow Jesus, while their son seems to be making his way back, with a hard road to travel.

Imagine my role as facilitator of the focus group. My stomach felt queasy as I anticipated the next question I was to ask: What would a successful transition look like for a Christian young person as he or she passed from adolescence to adulthood?

Seemingly, this question would force Mike and Michele to relive their heartbreak all over again while Tom and Alice would have to decide whether they could say anything without sounding like know-it-alls. Tom and Alice didn't seem the type to say, "Want to know what success looks like? Just look at our children!"

Reluctantly, I spit out my question. Then something remarkable happened. Alice, the mother of the five thriving kids said, "I don't think we could say our kids have successfully transitioned because they have never had their faith really tested. Our kids haven't gone through adversity—haven't faced any real trials the way Mike and Michele's kids have. I don't think we can say ours have yet made the transition to an adult Christian faith."

Here was a golden nugget in the midst of the mystery and messiness of raising Christ-following kids. Alice reflected the truth of Scripture: God uses trials of various kinds to refine our faith and our character. Alice concluded that her own children, though at a great place in life, still had a journey to travel. Alice came to this insight listening to Christian parents who had seen both their children end up on an entirely different plan than the one they imagined. And although Alice didn't say it directly, she reflected the biblical truth that the story hadn't yet ended for Mike and Michele's wayward kids.

This story is messy with all kinds of loose ends, and I have to leave it that way. I'd like to have a tidy package for you, but I don't. We can't know the future for Tom and Alice's kids. Nor can we know the future for Mike and Michele's kids. Here's what we can know: our God is full of steadfast love for us, our children, and the believing communities to which we belong. God has given us Scripture, brainpower, and experience that we might discover grace-filled pathways on which to walk. If we ask, God will give us guidance and wisdom regarding our individual children and specific circumstances as well.

THE NATIONAL STUDY OF YOUTH AND RELIGION

The National Study of Youth and Religion (NSYR) is a groundbreaking research project led by two sociologists, Christian Smith (Notre Dame) and Lisa Pearce (UNC-Chapel Hill). The NSYR research consisted of surveys and interviews conducted in three parts between 2001 and 2010. The purpose of the survey was to understand the religious beliefs, attitudes, and practices of teenagers and young adults, as well as to explore what (or who) influences these beliefs, attitudes, and practices.

While the study did not discover a single cure for the disaffection with the church and Christian faith so prevalent in the transition from ages eighteen to twenty-three, the NSYR did see a helpful pattern. When the six factors described below are present in the life of an eighteen-year-old, they are predictive of a successful transition. In other words, eighteen-year-olds whose lives align with the following list are much more likely to still be following Jesus at age twenty-three.

1. *The influence and example of highly religious parents* who regularly attend church and demonstrate that their faith is a high priority by the way they live on a daily basis.
2. *The high importance of religious faith for the teen*, a faith that is central to the teen's identity, even if the teen is marginalized for that faith by peers. The importance of faith for the teen might also show in regular attendance of church and possibly youth group.
3. *The teen has many religious experiences*, including a commitment to God, definite answers to prayer, a miracle, and one or more moving spiritual experiences.
4. *The teen frequently prays and reads Scripture.*
5. *The teen has many adults in a congregation to turn to for help and support.*
6. *The teen has few or no doubts about religious belief.*[1]

Forget the Formula, Search for Wisdom

If you are like me, you'd prefer a formula for raising emerging adults rather than just road signs or pathways that point in the right direction. Scripture, however, offers guidance, not formulae. Sometimes even the guidance is confusing.[2]

For example, how did Ecclesiastes, a book repeatedly proclaiming "Life is meaningless," make it into the canon of Scripture? Welcome to biblical wisdom literature. Fortunately, this is not the last word from Ecclesiastes, but like much of what we read in Job and at least part of Proverbs, the message in Ecclesiastes sobers us up in a hurry when we bring a cause-and-effect mentality to our ideas of righteous living.

"Life is not so simple," says the writer (paraphrased). In fact, "there are righteous people who are treated as if they did wicked deeds, and there are wicked people who are treated as if they did righteous deeds" (see Eccles. 8:14).

In the context of parenting, we might paraphrase as follows: "There are crappy parents who raise godly children and godly parents who raise rebellious children. God, what's up with that?!"

Important ideas from the rich world of biblical wisdom inform my thinking about helping our kids to follow Jesus into adulthood. As a broken human myself, and the parent of four emerging adults, I'm aware I have no godly right to pontificate about parenting. Sometimes as I write, I am painfully aware of this fact.

At the same time, I have reasonable hope that God will use the sources I've studied as well as the accounts I've been privileged to hear from parents, staff members, and students to guide both reader and writer as we explore our pivotal role as Christian parents. We have solid principles on which we can stand and act. As we explore those principles, I offer the following four truths from the biblical wisdom literature as a foundation:

1. *Wisdom is different from knowledge.* Knowing the truth about parenting (or anything else) is essential, but it is not

enough. We need to know how truth applies in everyday life in the midst of our own complex families, particularly as we raise children. For this, we need wisdom, which is the ability to respond to circumstances in the right way at the right time. People who are growing in wisdom are growing in the ability to read other people and use the truth of Scripture in appropriate ways. Prerequisites for growth in wisdom are humility and a teachable spirit. These are often opposed to the arrogance of the learned.

2. *Our gracious God is the only source of wisdom.* As parents, we aren't called to be perfect or even certain of how to handle every situation with every child. As parents, we are called to rely on God for daily wisdom, just as we are called to rely on him for daily bread.

> For the LORD grants wisdom!
> > From his mouth come knowledge and understanding.
> He grants a treasure of common sense to the honest.
> > He is a shield to those who walk with integrity.
> He guards the paths of the just
> > and protects those who are faithful to him. (Prov. 2:6–8 NLT)

3. *God is generous rather than stingy with wisdom.* Here is a glorious promise: "If any of you lacks wisdom, let him ask God, who gives generously to all without reproach, and it will be given him" (James 1:5 ESV).

4. *From the perspective of wisdom, parenting is a series of pathways, not a formula.* Wisdom teaches us to walk on the pathways of life with our children, avoiding those that lead to death.

Much of what I will introduce to you in the pages that follow will not work without wisdom. In fact, my aim is to introduce ways of thinking and acting that most readily lend themselves to wise decisions in the messy world of parenting. I'm trying to help build pathways, but you and your child will be the ones doing the walking, deciding whether to go slow or fast, where to turn, when to slow down, when to stop, and when it's time to turn around. I hope you will take this opportunity to join me in praying for wisdom.

Where Do We Go from Here?

To begin talking about the role of parents in the successful transition from adolescent to adult faith, we have to define a successful transition—at least for discussion purposes. Here's our working definition, informed by hundreds of thoughtful responses via a survey of CCO staff and interested adults: *The young adult Christian owns his or her faith in Jesus Christ, reflects it in priorities and decisions, and lives it in community with other believers, seeking to influence the watching world.*

If you find you don't fully agree with the definition, that's okay. We'll unpack the definition in chapter 2. After that, you can adapt the definition according to your own tradition and reading of the Scriptures. The important thing is to have a biblically informed picture of where you want your child to end up. Without a definition, the journey won't make much sense.

Throughout my research and experience, seven damaging myths emerged. I think of these as worn-out ways of thinking and acting. They are culturally generated and widely accepted beliefs. Acting, consciously or subconsciously, on any of these myths diminishes your parental influence in dangerous ways. I'll explore and debunk these myths in chapter 3.

In contrast to the culturally generated myths that threaten all of us, eight truths or principles emerged as I sifted through all my sources. These principles form the bedrock on which Christian parents can stand and act. They define the influence that is rightfully ours, and they tell us how to recapture it. Chapters 4 to 11 each explore one principle in depth. Each includes biblical guidance, sound research, and practical steps a parent can take to put love into action. Here is an overview of the eight principles.

1. Kids who make successful transitions don't have perfect parents who know everything.
2. Kids who successfully transition have parents who acknowledge their limits of control but still find ways to maintain their influence.
3. The home is still the greatest place of opportunity for shaping the faith of a young person and preparing him or her for a life beyond the home.
4. Kids who successfully transition have a bunch of loving grown-ups in their corner.
5. Kids who successfully transition learn to "keep good company" in high school and maintain the practice in college.
6. Faith *can* still thrive in an unfriendly place like college.
7. In youth as well as adulthood, difficulties and trials can lead to positive spiritual growth.
8. Kids who make bad choices need our love and support more than ever.

How to Use This Book

Recapture your sense of power. Pray for wisdom. Follow the principles. Trust that God, who gave you the incredible gift of a child, will be with you and that child even during the most turbulent times in life.

Read with hope, knowing God loves your child in a fierce and wonderful way, whether or not that child is walking with him right now. Read with arms open to receive grace, knowing that the whole burden of raising your child rests not on your broken shoulders but on him who is able to do abundantly more than we dare ask or think (see Eph. 3:20).

2

Getting Clear on the Goal

There seems to be something mildly inappropriate if not downright unspiritual about defining "success" for the Christian life at any age. Here is why it matters for the young people under your roof: you already have a definition for a successful result of the eighteen- to twenty-three-year-old transition. It may not be explicit, and you might have a hard time writing it down. You might never have reflected on it, but it is there somewhere below the surface: a set of expectations of what life would ideally be like for your post-college child if "things work out."

Let me give an example from my own family. My parents somehow communicated to my sisters, my brother, and me that our time at home was over when we received our college diplomas. Neither my siblings nor my mom or dad could remember even one conversation that directly dealt with the matter. No one said, "Son, you understand that your mother and I have lots of places to go and people to visit, and although we like you very much, we're not taking you along, so please plan accordingly."

How did we get the message from them so clearly? One possibility is that they were both Jedi Masters, using their "These aren't the droids you're looking for" skills to help us see a bright future living somewhere else.

In lieu of Jedi powers, there is the fact that my parents believed it was in our best interest to live independently of them when we became adults. This was embedded in their view of what a successful transition would look like, and so they parented based on this goal for years. They communicated what they deeply valued in all kinds of indirect ways, and the message came across as clearly as if they had told us point-blank.

We parents find a way to express our deepest convictions about things to our kids, even (and especially) when these convictions are never spoken aloud. Right now you have some hopes about the adult version of your son or daughter, whether or not you have written them down or discussed them with your spouse. Why not get clear about those hopes and make sure they are the ones you want to influence how you raise your child, whether he or she is twenty-one and starting to look for a job or fifteen and not even considering college?

We Christians have unwittingly adopted many of the same goals and standards for our children as the surrounding culture. The world around us is loud and persistent in declaring what success for twenty-three-year-olds is (material prosperity, good looks, sexual prowess). It is time that we dream together with our children about a different kind of future for them, one that reflects God's best for their lives.

Let's make Scripture our starting point for the conversation. Like any Christians, our sons and daughters come under the authority of the whole counsel of God from Genesis to Revelation. And so the admonitions we experience as we encounter God's Word apply as much to them as to us. See, for example, "Love one another. As I have loved you" (John 13:34), "Avoid sexual immorality," (1 Thess. 4:3), "Work . . . as for the Lord" (Col. 3:23 ESV), and "Do not be overcome by evil, but overcome evil with good" (Rom. 12:21). But a definition of success that says, "Obey the whole New Testament in every way," is not only a burden greater than we ourselves can bear; it doesn't fit the particular time and place in life God has called our kids.

For the purpose of our discussion, though, we need a definition, a target of sorts. The quest for a successful faith transition in our kids necessarily raises the question, "Transition to what?" This "what," target, or destination point cannot explicitly include every commandment and admonition from all of Scripture and is one we will not all agree on. What it should do is the following:

- Reflect the great commandments: "'Love the Lord your God with all your heart and with all your soul and with all your strength and with all your mind'; and 'Love your neighbor as yourself'" (Luke 10:27).
- Be undergirded by the gospel: "For it is by grace you have been saved, through faith—and this is not from yourselves, it is the gift of God—not by works, so that no one can boast" (Eph. 2:8–9).
- Be congruent with the practices of the earliest church: "They devoted themselves to the apostles' teaching and to fellowship, to the breaking of bread and to prayer" (Acts 2:42).

There is always more to learn about conforming our lives to the image of Jesus, about taking his good yoke on us, but the items listed above importantly provide a lifelong framework for continued growth as his children and his ambassadors to the world.

Given the challenge of creating a definition of success, I asked for help in the form of an online survey. The 310 men and women who responded are mostly, but not all, parents. Many have college-aged and young adult children and write from firsthand experience. Others have young children, and while they look forward to the uncharted territory of raising adolescents, they have much clearer memories of their own transitions to adulthood. Some are single and have never had kids of their own. All the respondents have a strong interest in the question of a "successful transition to an adult faith," and as you can see from the quotations in this chapter, many are thoughtful and passionate. I looked for repeated themes and discernible patterns in these responses and distilled them into what follows.

Here, then, is a definition of what we can hope for in the lives of our newly adult children (think ages twenty-three or twenty-four). Each of the three elements is followed by examples of parent and adult child responses from the survey.

1. They *own it*. It is not a parent's faith anymore; it is theirs. They will practice it independently of mother or father, and may go beyond them in its exercise. This ownership is rooted in his or her personal, real experience of God's presence and work, often in miraculous ways. It typically manifests itself in their desire to know God better through disciplines of prayer and Scripture reading.

> When they start agreeing with me! No, seriously, when they go beyond questioning to accepting, affirming and committing. Claiming the faith for their own.

> For me, personally, it happened on the other side of a faith crisis. Questions asked by secular professors in college dislodged what had been a very secure faith adopted from my mother. I had to scramble about, seek advice, and pray like crazy. After about a year, I came out on the other side, knowing that my faith—however unstable still—was my own.

> Similar to psychological development, spiritual/faith development benchmarks of "adulthood" are marked by the embrace of responsibility: to take ownership of one's growth—sole dependence on others becomes secondary.

> When he or she has accepted Christian faith as his or her own, rather than the faith of his or her parents or church, and can explain

and defend his or her basic beliefs. In other words, the person has internalized, personalized, and "owned" his faith.

2. It is a *consequential faith* (with thanks to Kenda Creasy Dean, who coined this phrase). A consequential faith permeates everything and is focused on God's mission to the world. It shows itself in a life oriented toward serving others and is integral to decision making—the choice of a job, spouse, neighborhood—and the setting of priorities.

> You see it by the choices they are making, the people they associate with, and how they deal with adversity. You see it in their conversation, conduct, and character.

> I stuck with the gospel even when it cost me something. The transition to adult faith can be recognized when individuals choose Christ and the life he calls us to over, against, and sometimes in the face of the life we once lived outside of Christ. Transition to adult faith is manifested out of the tension of having to make choices between building the empire of self or building the Kingdom of God.

> Many parts: 1. When they can move from "faith protects me from the world" to "faith transforms the world." 2. When they can balance loving Christ and loving the world (cosmos) at the same time. 3. When being in Christ (piety, prayer, worship, evangelism) also becomes being in the world (justice, mercy, excellence, discernment).

3. It is a *shared faith*. It is nurtured in Christian community, particularly the local church. It is a faith that—though deeply personal—is not deeply private but rather joyfully shared with those not yet possessing it.

> When he/she understands the call to minister in and to the world as part of the church rather than simply being the object of the church's ministry.

[When they] care enough about integrity of one's faith and the dignity of others to give faith away (i.e., it's no longer your "private" faith; commitment to discipleship and social/cultural transformation).

When, apart from parental presence, involvement, or influence, they bear witness to their faith in Christ in words, and begin to live life with a sense of personal devotion to, love for, and trust in Christ.

I think even questioning why parents attend a certain church or denomination is a healthy sign that a young adult has more than a superficial understanding of Christianity, but rather is interested in making their own faith tangible. (One of the first things our oldest did that made me realize that she truly loved the Lord apart from her father and I . . . before even filling out the college applications, she was looking for churches near the colleges where she could attend and volunteer . . . that was a big indicator for me! She recognized the importance of being in corporate worship and having a place to be accountable and also serve God's people . . . her words, not mine.) Whew . . . 1 down, 3 to go. Lol.

Once again, in one concise sentence, here is our working definition: *The young adult Christian owns his or her faith in Jesus Christ, reflects it in priorities and decisions, and lives it in community with other believers, seeking to influence the watching world.*

You may find this definition on target. You may also believe it contains too little, too much, or should be traded out for something else. Please use this definition as a starting point and feel free to give your own language to the God-induced longings you have for your child.

Serving Two Masters

Other visions of success compete with a kingdom of God goal: "Seek first the kingdom of God and his righteousness, and all these things will be added to you" (Matt. 6:33 ESV). Though many visions of success compete as well, let's examine one that has worked its way into the hearts of Christians in our age and in ages before us.

At the CCO, we work with all kinds of students from all walks of life. Even so, parents share some fundamental ideas about success for their kids. For example, I recently heard the story of a young man who attends a community college in the East. Paul not only has strong mechanical aptitude, but he loves doing work we typically think of as blue-collar. Paul's dad has done similar labor throughout his career, but he wants "better" for his son, which is clearly a white-collar (office) job. This push from blue- to white-collar is not unusual in an American context, as it is the life story of many families, sometimes worked out over multiple generations. Success is defined as moving up a job status ladder.

A different student, Elsa, attends an elite liberal arts university in the Midwest. Her family is wealthy and has given her access to the best: private education, private music lessons, additional coaching in sports, and a web of relationships with current and future people of influence. Elsa's parents have poured much time and energy, along with many resources, into their daughter so that she can live fully into her God-given abilities. They expect her education to ensure Elsa eventually lands a prestigious job and a secure financial future.

Nothing is inherently wrong with either of these scenarios on the surface. What parents don't want their children to have a life they, the parents, perceive to be better than their own? Shouldn't we all want to help our kids live into their potential? Isn't that what the parable of the talents is all about ("Use 'em or lose 'em")?

As we think of Paul, Elsa, and the myriad emerging adults they represent, we must carefully define the highest level of success. In the event of a conflict, which is more important? The success, stability, and prosperity you see in your child's future, or seeking first God's kingdom in all they do? One must be preeminent—they cannot both be top dog. The same is true of a successful marriage match and other healthy goals.

I'm not suggesting we shouldn't want our kids to be economically self-sufficient (Oh happy day!) or even capable of generating wealth. In my role with the CCO, I spend a lot of time with well-off people, many of whom love and serve Jesus in ways I can only dream about. But hear the words of Jesus regarding the affections of the heart: "No one can serve two masters. Either you will hate the one and love the other, or you will be devoted to the one and despise the other. You cannot serve both God and money" (Luke 16:13).

As parents, we must examine the messages we project to our kids about success, especially those we communicate without words. This is particularly true as we send our kids to college or to work, because so many priorities clamor for their attention. We may say Jesus is top dog and then undermine our own words in favor of good grades, suitable spouses, and prestigious careers.

This message is as challenging to me as to anyone. I want a prosperous, comfortable life. I have tasted the good life, and I want more! And I want at least the same for our four kids. God have mercy on me!

Encourage your kids to explore and develop their abilities, to learn what is excellent and praiseworthy, to work with all their hearts "as for the Lord" (Col. 3:23 ESV). Please be clear in your example and your words, though, that you hold worldly success and its trappings loosely. Be openhanded, generous, fully devoted to the Lord Jesus Christ, and help your kids to do the same. Serve the real master, not a counterfeit one.

Perhaps the love of money and the status that comes with money are not your primary temptations. But for most of us (okay, for all of us) *something* pulls at us, eagerly offering itself as a substitute for that which is freely available: the very life of God. To understand what will tug on our kids, we should consider what tugs on us. The desire for comfort apart from conflict is an ongoing struggle for me. I've known families that elevate dating relationships and marriage to the place of an idol. From this starting place, parents communicate to their kids that having a girlfriend or boyfriend is what makes life worth living.

In other cases, the idol is creating significance through athletic performance. Sports are a powerful force in our culture, apart from unresolved issues with sports we might have had when we were growing up. But what if we combine the cultural idol of athletic accomplishment with an itch we could never quite scratch when we were kids? "I could have been a great point guard if I had just worked a little harder." Take what we disproportionately value as a society and add our own unmet needs (needs that will only find their answer when we are reconciled to God), and you can produce a toxic set of priorities for your kids.

The same could be said for academic achievement, social popularity, food, or any number of other draws. Notice that each is a good thing—part of what God gives us to steward and enjoy—but none work well for us or for our kids as the ultimate thing. When we serve anything or anyone apart from God, we have set up ourselves and our children for disappointment.

What Would Be Different?

Consider the working definition of transition success one more time: *The young adult Christian owns his or her faith in Jesus Christ, reflects it in priorities and decisions, and lives it in community with other believers, seeking to influence the watching world.*

Now ask yourself, "How would I parent differently if I were doing so with this definition of success in mind?" It might be helpful to think along two different, but related paths. One path is the one your child is walking. Are the experiences they are having and the people with whom they are surrounded likely to build their faith, connect them to the body of Christ, and give them a heart for others? Or are they learning it is all about them?

31

The second path is yours, and it is probably the more powerful of the two. Are you living in a way that demonstrates, however imperfectly, a genuine, consequential faith in Jesus? Don't lay yourself low with the need to be perfect, but consider what someone who watches you from a close distance may conclude about what you value the most.

You may want a definition of a successful faith transition different from what I've come up with here. Feel free to capture it in your own words and test it against the Scriptures and the wisdom of other Christians. What's important is letting a godly target influence how you live and encourage your children to live.

Read on, and as you do, keep in mind this definition as if it were a destination point on a trip.

The next chapter should help you eliminate some routes that, although they are well traveled, are pretty well guaranteed to take you and your child just where you don't want to go.

3

Seven Myths That Might Be Sabotaging Your Parenting

When it comes to finding out what is crooked about your own culture, gaining the perspective from someone outside of it can help. Here is what Chido, a college student originally from Nigeria, has observed about the American college experience: "For some reason, everyone just expects college students to behave recklessly."

Chido has his finger on the pulse of what we might call the "Sowing Wild Oats Myth," which is the belief that crazy, risky behavior is necessary to fulfill some kind of secret coming-of-age requirement. "Better to get it out of the youngster's system," we can hear a well-meaning family member say. Who decided sowing wild oats is a necessary element of growing up in America? Because it is not that way in all cultures.

Chido understands that what we think—the beliefs we hold as true—drive the choices we make. "A mind really is a terrible thing to waste!" Chido says, paraphrasing the old slogan from the United

Negro College Fund. In Chido's thinking, a mind is useless (or worse) when it acts from assumptions that are not true.

For example, if we think our adolescent child won't listen to us, we stop talking with her. Once we stop talking, of course the child stops seeking out our counsel. How can it be otherwise?

We act on what we think and believe until our thoughts and convictions become reality. We subconsciously behave in ways that reinforce our belief system. If our society sends limitless messages to college-aged students that young adult years are for sowing wild oats, they will act on this belief—unless we, as Christian parents, can counter the messages with biblical truth and a measure of common sense.

As parents, myth-busting is one of the most worthy exercises in which we can engage. We need to sift through the messages society sends our children, reinforcing those that support biblical teaching and growth into mature faith. We need to clearly and consistently debunk those that don't. The starting place is the space between our own ears, where we may currently be captive to a bit of what Zig Ziglar calls that "stinkin' thinkin'."

In my research and experience, seven myths, or "worn-out ways of thinking and acting," show up repeatedly. Each pertains to raising kids who will own and live their Christian faith as adults.

Myth 1: Parents are peripheral in the lives of emerging adults.

Myth 2: Christian professionals (not parents) have the primary responsibility for the spiritual nurture of emerging adults.

Myth 3: College is a time for emerging adults to sow their wild oats.

Myth 4: It is unrealistic to expect college students to attend church regularly.

Myth 5: Christian faith has no place in an intellectually rigorous environment such as college.

Myth 6: Saying it is enough.

Myth 7: "I've got a good kid!"

Myth 1: Parents are peripheral in the lives of emerging adults.

Do you remember what the adults sound like in the Peanuts made-for-television specials? It's sort of a "wah wah wah" sound made by a trombone with a plunger mute. Is that how parents sound to their teenage kids? Or is it the sound made popular by the TV show *Seinfeld*, "yadda yadda yadda"? Let's find out what the evidence actually suggests about the role of parents in the life of Christian teenagers.

Several years ago, Notre Dame professor and researcher Christian Smith led a team that conducted the National Study of Youth and Religion (NSYR), seeking to understand the religious and spiritual lives of emerging adults, that is, those in the eighteen- to twenty-three-year-old category. Smith's research actually begins with this same group as thirteen- to seventeen-year-olds, so his data is particularly useful for those raising the questions we are asking here.[1]

The results show a cluster of factors that show up in the lives of teens and then again in young adult believers. Looking at just four of these six factors is somewhat predictive. Sixty-eight percent of teens with the following characteristics have a significantly engaged faith as young adults:

- highly religious parents
- high importance of religious faith as teens
- many personal religious experiences
- frequent praying and reading of Scripture

As Smith puts it, for the eighteen- to twenty-three-year-old age range, "The forces of religious continuity are stronger than the forces of change."[2]

This finding contrasts markedly with what average American parents believe about their influence over their young adult children.

Those of us in the church seem to buy into the same belief without questioning. Here is how Smith puts it:

> When teenagers send signals to "Get out of my life," many parents seem all too ready to comply, even if with mixed emotions. In short, most Americans have swallowed hook, line, and sinker the "Parents of teenagers are irrelevant" myth. . . . Oddly, this withdrawal of parental influence on adolescents seems most especially evident when it comes to religious commitments and practices. . . . Thus, in the name of individual autonomy—informed here by a cultural myth that is sociologically erroneous—the usually most crucial players in teenagers' lives disengage from them precisely when they most need conversation partners to help sort through these weighty matters.[3]

Can you imagine any of us purposely ignoring one of our kids if he or she is in pain or needs our help? That's what Smith is describing here. Kids do want to have that conversation, or as Smith says later, "They simply want that input and engagement on renegotiated grounds that take seriously their growing maturity and desired independence."[4]

If Myth 1 is that beginning with adolescence, parents are irrelevant, Myth 2 naturally follows for Christian families.

Myth 2: Christian professionals (not parents) have the primary responsibility for the spiritual nurture of emerging adults.

Although church and parachurch professionals are enormously important in leading our kids to Jesus and helping them grow in their faith, the home is still the center of spiritual nurture.

Here is what Scripture says about teaching our kids God's Word (his commands):

> You shall teach them to your children, talking of them when you are sitting in your house, and when you are walking by the way, and when you lie down, and when you rise. (Deut. 11:19 ESV)

Beginning with our kids' infancy, we parents spend enormous amounts of time with them, and so we have the opportunity to help them learn God's ways in the context of everyday life—hour by hour, day by day, year after year. Your pastor and your youth pastor are acutely aware of the limited amount of time they have to shape your kids (and shape you!).

Mom, Dad, you have this opportunity in a way no one else does. It is not only a great privilege but a serious responsibility—we don't have the option to defer our central role for the spiritual nurture of our kids to another person or another institution. Youth workers and the church are there to help, not take the place of parents. We will talk more about this weighty privilege (it is a privilege!) later, but for now, let's name the myth and move on.

Myth 3: College is a time for emerging adults to sow their wild oats.

"Seven years of college down the drain" was a hilarious line when scripted into the movie *Animal House*, but the concept is not nearly so funny in real life, particularly if you are the one paying tuition!

The "college students will sow wild oats" myth holds a certain allure for those of us who take our fun seriously. But consider this: First, this assumption is supported nowhere in Scripture. In fact, the most memorable wild oat sower of all is the prodigal son, for whom such a condition is to run from, not to embrace. Second, I have seen the damage in the life of a young person who makes one very bad decision or gets stuck in a pattern of self-destructive behavior or even addiction. Third, I talk to many adults with deep regrets about things they did during a period of wild oat sowing. It sounds fun, but this myth belongs with the rest of them.

It also brings to memory the sound of my shoes sticking to the beer patina on the slate floor of my frat house as I headed out for church on Sunday morning. Which introduces the next myth.

Myth 4: It is unrealistic to expect college students to attend church regularly.

If home and the family are central to the spiritual nurture of children, the church is essential. This is where we take the Lord's Supper together, a sacrament all Christians share in and that powerfully communicates God's grace. Church is also a place of instruction and exhortation (preaching), a place where God is worshiped, and the setting where Christians are guaranteed to connect with other Christ-followers.

For college students, it is a chance to be with people who are not eighteen to twenty-three years old. In the CCO's work with students, we regularly see the magic that can happen when students engage in the life of the church.

This is some of the "why" of college church attendance. It still begs the question, "Is it realistic to expect a college kid, who has stayed up until who-knows-when, to make it to a Sunday morning service?" Thousands do every week! What follows are two examples. More will be in chapter 9.

Consider Graystone Presbyterian Church in Indiana, Pennsylvania (yes, such a place exists, and it is the childhood home of the greatest actor ever, Jimmy Stewart), home of Indiana University of Pennsylvania, a state school of about fifteen thousand students.

Graystone looks like a church: stone (more of a tan than gray, actually), stained glass, pews, an altar, the whole thing. Most weeks during the school year, students occupy the first four or five pews across the front of the church. Students are in the chancel choir and they are part of workdays. When Graystone recently left its historic denomination, much of the choir left Graystone. College students saw the need and responded, more than twenty showing up for the choir at 8:30 on Sunday morning.

Church members feed students lunch every week, invite them into their homes, mentor them, and consciously do things together, such as mission trips. On the Sunday before the CCO's annual

Jubilee Conference, most of the sixty-eight students who would be attending were commissioned in front of the whole church. Isn't that a poignant picture of what we want to see happen in the lives of students?

Consider Christ Community Church of the South Hills (CCCSH) and its CCO outreach to Point Park University. Point Park is a downtown Pittsburgh school known for the performing arts that has three CCO staff who are in partnership with two churches in addition to CCCSH.

CCCSH, unlike Graystone, meets in a school gym. The worship experience is informal and contemporary. And it is twelve miles from the Point Park campus, which means students have to go to extraordinary lengths to get there on Sunday mornings. But get there they do as part of the congregation, worship band, and so on. CCCSH members reciprocate. They are on campus on a weekly basis for fellowship meetings, special events, or just some time with students they know. Several years ago the church changed the dates for its annual mission trip so students could use their spring break to go along.

One note here for kids who have grown up with powerful church experiences in high school: it is important to acknowledge that they will not find a church just like their church at home when they are in college. I'm sure this is used as a convenient excuse sometimes ("I can't find a church as good as ours"), but regardless, it is important for some kids to be alerted to this going in.

For parents, I strongly encourage you to back off your preferences, particularly if they are denominational. Keep in mind that the church of your "brand" might not exist in the community where your son or daughter is headed, and if it does it might not be the best place to worship, learn, and serve. Let me go out on a limb here and say a few words to Catholic moms and dads.

Among Christian denominations, Roman Catholic young people are statistically having a rougher transition than almost any other group, with more than 80 percent leaving the church during college.

Because of the teachings and practices of the Catholic Church, Catholic parents are reticent to recommend alternatives even if the Catholic church near campus is especially uninspiring. You may want to look at options that are still Catholic but don't look like the home parish. At the University of Pittsburgh, for example, there is an Oratory at the edge of campus that is a worshiping Catholic community and is connected to the Newman Center. Penn State hosts regular masses on campus, as do many other schools. Vibrant, excellent Catholic student movements are at campuses all over the country, many of which are also attended by post-college adults who make the campus church their parish.

But if it is a choice between attending a non-Catholic church that feeds the faith of your child or dropping out of Christianity altogether, I would counsel you to be open to the former.

For all Christian parents, set an expectation with your child that includes becoming part of a church.

Myth 5: Christian faith has no place in an intellectually rigorous environment such as college.

The pervasiveness of this myth is evidenced by what we often hear from unchurched students: "I thought being a Christian meant checking your mind at the door." Ouch! When the Barna Group researched the attitudes of those alienated from the Christian faith they found that many believed Christians were "anti-science."[5] Where do these popularly held ideas come from?

First, they come from inside the church. Many Christians, particularly evangelicals, have an uneasy relationship with the life of the mind. When Mark Noll published *The Scandal of the Evangelical Mind* in 1995, he noted the failure of evangelical Protestantism to, among other things, treat science, art, politics, and social analysis with the seriousness that God intends.[6] The problem is that college is very much about the "life of the mind": science, art, politics, social analysis, literature, and so on.

40

Second, the surrounding, prevailing culture does not see faith and intellectual pursuit as compatible. Facts exist in one realm and faith in another, never to meet. And so Christians are often assumed to be folks who can't handle reality and who are part of something that will die away as scientific discoveries supplant the need for belief in a supreme being.

So if we are steeped in a tradition that is suspicious of intellectual inquiry, and surrounded by a culture that reinforces this belief, we might not send our kids into a place of intellectual rigor with all that much confidence.

What do you believe? As you are "sitting in your house" and "walking by the way," what attitudes toward learning, discovery, and the life of the mind are you modeling? Is it an approach rooted in fear or in confidence? Our forebears believed the words of Colossians 1:16 that the whole cosmos (universe) was made by, through, and for Jesus Christ. As a result, they were not afraid but eager to learn about every part of God's good creation they could grasp.

Myth 6: Saying it is enough.

The essence of this myth is captured in a cliché: "Actions speak louder than words," or as Ralph Waldo Emerson put it, "What you do speaks so loudly that I cannot hear what you say." What's true for any human being is inescapable for those in visible positions of authority, such as teachers, business leaders, pastors, and parents. You might be heard (or not!), but you will certainly be watched!

I believe this is magnified in families because we are around each other so much. You can't fake it under your own roof. I don't remember my dad talking about the importance of forgiveness until I was grown and someone asked him, but I do remember him forgiving my many, many offenses (I was a bad kid for a spell) and allowing our relationship to start with a clean slate.

Shame researcher Brené Brown points out[7] that helping a kid not to feel ashamed when he/she spills milk ("It's what you did; it is not who you are") doesn't do much good if they see us use shame when we talk to ourselves ("You are such a doofus!").

What are your kids learning about following Jesus by watching you?

Myth 7: "I've got a good kid!"

The world and the church will reward us if we raise kids who seem considerate of others, are reasonably polite, and avoid doing bad things. And they should—these are great attributes, along with those other personal conduct items we used to have on our report cards such as "personal hygiene," "shows self-control" and "plays well with others." I feel happy when I see one of our kids exhibiting this kind of good behavior. It's just not the ultimate thing. The goal in Christian faith is inner transformation, not merely behavior modification. The question is, "Am I focused right now on my child's actions or the heart behind those actions?"

When David was being sorted out from all of his bigger, stronger siblings, God told the prophet Samuel, "Man looks on the outward appearance, but the LORD looks on the heart" (1 Sam. 16:7 ESV). Isn't looking to outward appearances a primary temptation for Christians—the very issue over which Jesus fought with religious leaders? "Woe to you, teachers of the law and Pharisees, you hypocrites! You clean the outside of the cup and dish, but inside they are full of greed and self-indulgence. Blind Pharisee! First clean the inside of the cup and dish, and then the outside also will be clean" (Matt. 23:25–26). A child who has all the external trappings of being "a good kid" but lacks any real experience of God might or might not grow into a "good adult." How does this fit with your definition of a successful transition?

Which Myths Hit Home for You?

Do you see yourself or your family reflected in any of these myths? You are not alone! Perhaps you can add to the list I've come up with here. A myth begins to die when we can name it. Tales that are not quite true begin to lose their power when we recognize them for what they are. So if you see your own tendencies anywhere, you have already begun to do good work.

We are just getting started! The next chapters will help you identify what you can do now to get ready for launch, beginning with something you probably haven't heard much about: how being an imperfect parent is an asset, not a liability.

4

You Are Nowhere Close to Being a Perfect Parent

That's Okay

Every year, I brace myself against Christmas letters that go something like this:

> In between mission trips to the three most dangerous places in the world, Timmy finally solved the cold fusion problem, just in time to be crowned Homecoming King, release his new single (look for the video on YouTube), and lead two hundred of his peers in prayer at the "See You At The Pole" gathering. We just wish he were old enough to drive!

As parents, we know our kids' choices, accomplishments, and shortcomings reflect upon us. We want our own children to be versions of the stellar kids in other families' annual Christmas letters. The temptation to look good is particularly strong when we come to church. As "religious" people, we want others to think we have it together. As a result, we fall into the trap of parenting by appearance, not by the work of God in the hearts of our kids. This may bring to mind the "good kid" myth of the prior chapter.

When our children don't measure up to the appearances we think others expect, we feel inadequate, guilty, and ashamed. We sink into isolation rather than into community. Yet only in community can we build up each other.

No matter what the Christmas letter says, no family is as together as it appears. In fact, the "good kid" myth is a near neighbor to the "perfect parent" fantasy. No kid slides into admirable adulthood without struggle, and no parent fails to screw up on a regular basis. The imperfections may be hidden, but they are there.

Perhaps those who suffer most unjustly from the duplicity we perpetuate in the church are parents whose imperfections are not easy to hide. For example, those who have nonbelieving spouses, who are divorced, or who have trouble holding a job often feel the eyes of judgment upon them. And parents whose kids refuse to attend church or struggle with school or with addictions feel the heavy burden of imperfection, even when the church preaches grace.

If you are a parent whose imperfections are difficult to hide, take heart. If you are a parent who has made a big mistake that is affecting your kids, take heart. And if you are a parent who regularly screws up because you frequently don't know the right thing to do, take heart. Both biblical teaching and research proclaim this welcome truth: your child's successful transition to adult Christian faith does *not* depend on you getting everything just right.

Meet the McIntyre family. Their now-adult daughter, Libby, is the kind of young woman we would be proud to call our own: deeply devoted to Jesus Christ, an advocate for the poor, and married to an awesome Christian man. She is the only child of two remarkable parents, who continue to pour time into the children of their community, years after their own daughter has grown and left home.

Some time ago, I learned that Pete, Libby's dad, is an alcoholic. He self-medicated for a number of years, drinking himself to sleep on a daily basis and causing plenty of heartache for his wife and daughter. Pete is in a recovery group, and his wife and daughter are both in Al-Anon, a group birthed by Alcoholics Anonymous to aid family members of alcoholics. Pete has chosen to be open about his struggles, realizing that many in his community have a similar Achilles' heel. He is a friend and advocate to other men with addiction issues.

In contrast, meet the Bensons. Jim and Patty are the kind of people I want to be when I grow up. They are devoted followers of Christ, living into the axiom "God first, others second, and me third." Jim and Patty differ from each other in temperament—Jim is outgoing and transparent and Patty is quiet, shy, and gentle—but either would be a good choice if life were hard and you were down to one friend.

Right now, neither of Jim and Patty's kids, one an adolescent, one a young adult, is walking with God. Not every choice the Benson kids make is life-threatening or even foolish, but to an outsider, it is disquieting to watch them choose a path so different from their parents' path.

Sometimes, the best we can do as humans is to live within the tension of two seemingly irreconcilable truths. We have tremendous influence on the kinds of people our children become. And yet, we can do everything right—spend lots of time with our kids, surround them with wonderful Christian influences, saturate their lives with God's Word, model godliness and joy in our own lives—and still have things go way off course. Conversely, we can feel doomed by a besetting sin of some kind and see God somehow reach our kids in spite of (or because of) our own brokenness.

Earlier this year our local paper carried an article written by a mom who was keen to see her Jewish faith passed on to her son, who had enrolled at a large state university. In her tradition, faith was passed down through the mother more than the father, so as the family car approached campus, the question kept coming to her mind, "Did I do enough?"[1] The same question bedevils many a parent: "Have I done enough?"

This question is unanswerable, so leave it alone. Worry and guilt about the past has power to give you stomach ulcers, but it can make no difference in your child's life. What might begin to make a difference? For a Christian, few things are more powerful than getting the biblical story right.

Examine the Parental Role Models in Scripture

I recently saw a book titled *Shocked by the Bible*, which seeks to bust preconceived ideas about what is actually in the pages of Scripture. If you truly want to be "shocked" and would like an unfiltered look at some really dysfunctional families, read the Bible! What a mess.

Abraham is the father of our faith. To this man, together with his wife, Sarah, God made the promise to become "the father of many nations" (Gen. 17:4), with descendants who would be as numerous (as beyond counting) as "the stars in the sky and the sand on the seashore" (Gen. 22:17). So what kind of man was Abraham?

The story begins in Genesis 12. Abraham was brave. It took guts to leave his home city, Haran, and strike out on a journey to a place he knew little about. Abraham was resourceful and believed God, even when God's instructions seemed to make no sense. The biggest test of Abraham's faith came when God instructed Abraham to take his son Isaac to the top of a mountain to sacrifice as an offering. We know that in the end, God provided a substitute offering and so Isaac was spared. But it was an excruciating three-day journey to reach the top of the mountain. Imagine what that would have been like! Somehow, Abraham seems to know that God will come through: "God himself will provide the lamb for the burnt offering, my son" (Gen. 22:8).

Abraham was compassionate. Most people know about God's destruction of Sodom and Gomorrah. It was a wicked place, loaded not only with sexual predators but also with those who had little regard for the "poor and needy" (Ezek. 16:49). Abraham pleads for his nephew Lot and other residents in the two cities by bargaining with God, kind of like an auctioneer, but in descending order. "Will you spare the city if there are fifty righteous folks living there? How about forty-five? Forty? Do I hear . . . ten?" (See Gen. 19:16–33.)

Abraham was also a screwup. He was a liar. Two times in his travels he told locals that his wife, Sarah, was actually his sister (see Gen. 14:13; 20:2). This may have saved his neck, but it made Sarah vulnerable to becoming part of a potentate's harem. As Abraham and Sarah continued to age to a point beyond Sarah's childbearing years, it looked as if the promised heir would never come. Abraham acceded to Sarah's wishes for him to sleep with her servant, Hagar (see Gen. 16:1–2). The decision nearly blew their family apart and created an antagonism between Hagar's family (Ishmael/Ismail is considered the father of Arab peoples) and his own (as father of the Jews) that has lived on throughout history.

Sarah is not off the hook as our spiritual mother. Like Abraham, she demonstrated a lion's share of courage, faith, and resilience. Sarah, though, gets caught in mocking laughter when God tells her she will miraculously become pregnant (and then be the mother of a mighty nation, see Gen. 18:10–15). After Sarah's own son, Isaac, is born, she resents the presence of her servant Hagar and Hagar's son, Ishmael, who was conceived only after Sarah asked Abraham to sleep with Hagar. Sarah asks her husband (commands him, really) to send Hagar and Ishmael away, into the surrounding desert (see Gen. 21:8–14).

Generations later, we meet David, the great king of the Hebrew nation. David's good qualities are well documented, but his failures are enormous, particularly on the family front. He sleeps with the wife of one of his most loyal warriors and then has that man killed to cover the crime. If you are keeping a scorecard, that would be one case of adultery and one of cold-blooded, premeditated murder. As an older man, David coddles his wicked son, Absalom, who betrays his father and nearly brings down the kingdom.

We often think of biblical figures as wearing halos, but Scripture doesn't. It would have been easy for the inspired writers to edit out the crappy parts of the biographical accounts in Scripture. But here are stories of biblical parents—three-dimensional human beings, full of the best and worst human parents bring to the table. Chances are God shares these details with us in Scripture because the human parents are decidedly not the main characters in God's redemptive work. God is the main character, the only true hero in Scripture.

Each of the characters described above is used by God to do something extraordinary in history: to build God's kingdom and pave the way for the great reconciler/restorer, Jesus. Do you think you are worse than these guys? Really? If they aren't disqualified from service, neither are you!

Men and women from messed-up families are still eligible for kingdom leadership. What a wonderful relief!

Embrace Your Imperfections and Limitations

What would happen for us and for our children if we shifted our view about our failures? What if we stopped treating failures (ours and our kids') as embarrassments to hide and began to think of them as training ground for grace?

What would it mean to parents and kids if we welcomed them in from the cold, loving them in spite of mistakes and bad choices, praying with them, and, in the case of the parents, showing that we are in no position to judge?

The beginning point is acknowledging our own shortcomings. What's in your junk drawer: some envy, lust, perhaps a bit of greed, maybe a touch of bitterness? In chapter 11 we'll look more closely at God's heart toward screwups, but for now, let's note that God can really go to work with parents who are aware of their own wrongdoings and insufficiencies.

Remember, too, that neither our children nor we are finished products. We are in a process called sanctification, which means to "become holy." You and I will die before this process is anywhere near completion. In his great chapter on love, 1 Corinthians 13, the apostle Paul compares our comprehension of God to a person looking at themselves in a mirror. We see, but only dimly.

Paul, who looks so much like a fully mature Christian, is the one who laments his own unfinished-ness in Romans 7, wishing he could stop doing the stuff he wasn't supposed to do and start doing what he should. Like a man at a 12-step program, Paul acknowledges his own inability to change ("Wretched man that I am! Who will deliver me from this body of death?" [v. 24 ESV]) until it leads him to the entryway of God's grace: "Thanks be to God, who delivers me through Jesus Christ our Lord!" (v. 25 ESV).

Like Paul, we are on a journey, and, if we are blessed to have children, they too are fellow pilgrims. It is appropriate to be grieved by our own sins and shortcomings, but we should never really be surprised. We certainly don't need to be stuck, given that we have the opportunity to ask God's forgiveness and start over.

So instead of pretending perfection to ourselves and our kids, let's open a window, appropriately, to show how God works with us in our failings, fears, dreams, confusion, and relationships.

Imperfection and Hypocrisy

When we are willing to show it, imperfection is an antidote for hypocrisy. David Kinnaman, Gabe Lyons, and the Barna Group conducted research among young people who were alienated from the church. Their findings, published in the book *UnChristian*, reveal six things in the church that alienate sixteen- to twenty-six-year-olds (and undoubtedly others). These folks perceive church members as follows:

1. Hypocritical.
2. Too focused on getting converts.
3. Antihomosexual.
4. Sheltered.

5. Too political.

6. Judgmental.[2]

Unfortunately, the research shows that the perceptions developed more often than not from firsthand experiences the young men and women had with Christians and the church, not from messages filtered by the media.

We may be tempted to think our kids will not respect us if we admit to failures and weaknesses. Real damage, it appears, is done when we try to cover our sins and shortcomings with that "we have it all together in this family" veneer. Dealing honestly with the failings we show under our own roofs can stick a spear right through hypocrisy's heart.

A Community of the Imperfect

In my leadership role at the CCO, I've twice had the privilege to hike the Tour de Mont Blanc (TMB), a trail in the Alps that circumnavigates Europe's highest mountain and passes through three countries: France, Italy, and Switzerland. Members of the CCO Experiential Design team capably lead the trip, called the "Alpine Pilgrimage." It is a trek of fairy-tale beauty, complete with alpine meadows full of flowers, rushing rivers, and plenty of snow.

For most participants, this is a physically demanding hike. Out of eight days or so on the trail, we each will have at least one moment when our body, our mind, or both say, "Enough!" The problem is, of course, that we need to keep going. Stop, and we will spend the night shivering on the mountain.

I've trained for these hikes, eaten properly (mostly), and have done all I can to be ready. I am prepared and I am being well led, but that's not what gets me up that hill, over that pass, and down the other side. That task is left to my fellow pilgrims. Fellow hikers may do something tangible, such as transferring the giant jar of Nutella out of my pack to theirs or helping repair a blister on

CHRISTIAN FAITH REDEFINED: ONE COLLEGE STUDENT'S STORY

As an eighteen-year-old, I thought I knew what it meant to be a Christian. God was a distant figure of some power who sent Jesus primarily as an example of what it meant to love God and other people. My job as a human was to do what God wanted and to avoid what he didn't want. I saw the Christian faith primarily as a matter of self-discipline—rigorously governing thought, actions, and emotions in a God-pleasing way.

Here was the problem: it wasn't working. If the long-term project was learning to love God and others, I was going to need several millennia worth of personal growth to make it happen. That was if I didn't go backward. Going backward was a real possibility, because it seemed that the more self-disciplined I was, the more judgmental, impatient, and intolerant I was of other people.

During my freshman year my brother Dave convinced me to attend something called Jubilee, a conference for college students, still held every year in Pittsburgh. At Jubilee, a speaker named Tom Skinner disassembled what I thought I knew about the Christian faith with statements such as, "The worst sin you can commit is trying to be a Christian on your own power." Skinner had been a gang member in Harlem and now wanted everyone to have the same kind of encounter with Jesus that had so changed him.

That weekend I learned about a way to follow Jesus rooted in total forgiveness and total surrender. My failing self-improvement project died, and I became a new creation in Christ, still deeply imperfect but with new hope, new desires, and the knowledge that whatever happened in life, I would still be God's beloved child.

one of my feet. They may have direct words of encouragement, but more likely they will simply provide company. They may not say a word, but the fact that fellow travelers are with me, that we are huffing and puffing together up this steep hill, is enough.

When it comes time each evening to celebrate the day—the beauty, the accomplishment, the funny stuff that happened—these same fellow pilgrims are what makes that good French food and wine taste that much better. In both the difficulty and the sweetness of the journey, my fellow pilgrims bring both solace and joy.

So it is for Christ-following parents. We are on a long, sometimes arduous walk. We will have both moments of inexpressible joy (holding that infant for the first time) and times when we are just *done*, when our whole being cries out, "Enough!" If we are on this journey, we will need to link with other travelers headed for the same destination.

As you read this, take pen and paper, tablet, or laptop, and do a quick inventory of those with whom you and your spouse are making the parenting pilgrimage. Who is doing this with you? Who is willing to walk the hard road, even to the point of carrying stuff from your pack and allowing you to carry what they have in theirs?

If this exercise paints a rich picture of community, that is wonderful! Ask yourself one more question: Am I vulnerable enough with these people (are we as husband and wife?) to allow them to help me when I am hurting? You may be adjacent to loving brothers and sisters in Christ who can do little to support you because you are busy projecting "I have it all together." Take a risk and let these loving folks know when you are dispirited or defeated.

If your inventory shows only a thin line of support, or maybe none at all, recognize that you live in a day and age of lonely, isolated people. Strange as it sounds, you have lots of company in your isolation!

If you are not particularly well connected to a Christian community, I suggest a couple of options:

1. Investigate your church's small group ministry. Close relationships are not built with three hundred other people, so many churches facilitate groups of six to twelve people who can go deeper with each other. If you are in a small group that doesn't seem to openly share both trials and victories, then ask yourself why. Does your group feel like a safe place to be vulnerable? If it does, be more open; if not, find a new group.

2. Look for Christian friends in the normal course of your life: neighbors, co-workers, fellow school volunteers, other church members, and so on. God usually plants people around us who are potential fellow-pilgrims.

The Calling of Imperfect Parents

God does not ask us to be examples of perfection (trust me, it's above your pay grade). Nor does he expect us to wallow in our brokenness. Our job is to act as arrows pointing to God. Your life, in all of its messiness, can be just such an arrow. Remember what we see in the biblical story: your screwups do not disqualify you from kingdom leadership. Your screwups can present your most powerful teaching moments. What opportunities can you take as an imperfect parent?

1. Confess wrongs you commit against family members and others (more on this in the chapter on the home and the gospel).
2. Give and receive forgiveness, the need for which would not arise if you (and others) were perfect.
3. Model how to respond rightly to failure, which most humans eventually experience (unless they are hopelessly shallow).
4. Model the perseverance to finish something (like writing a book!), even when you know it isn't perfect.
5. Show grace to the other imperfect parent in your home.
6. Allow your imperfection to shape how you treat others.
7. Put the glory of God on display (see 2 Cor. 4:7) by being a cracked (read: imperfect) vessel that holds the treasure of God's presence.
8. Demonstrate humility. God really, truly does oppose the proud. The dents and dings of our imperfection are God's gift to keep us aware of our need for grace. They also remind us of who belongs on the throne.

9. Show that it is okay not to be good at everything.

10. Appreciate the God-given gifts of others.

11. Learn that God often shows himself strongest in our weakness: "My grace is sufficient for you, for my power is made perfect in weakness" (2 Cor. 12:9).

12. Relieve our kids from the pressure of living with other humans who are perfect.

This is a partial list. What would you add? What has been your experience with bringing your own brokenness and vulnerability to the work of being a mom or dad? How would you describe the calling of imperfect parents?

I've been a Christian since I was in college, for thirty-six years, and I recognize the place for disciplines (notice how easily that word becomes *disciple*) such as self-control and self-denial. But two other realities are at work, one from experience and one from Scripture:

1. I can't even begin to follow Jesus unless he is constantly changing me from the inside out (even self-discipline is a gift from him).

2. Jesus's nemeses were religious people. In the Gospels, particularly Mark, we see Jesus loving sinners and fighting with religious people.

The gospel, then, should deeply inform every part of our lives, perhaps most of all our roles as spouses and parents. On this side of heaven you will never be perfect. This means you will never treat your kids exactly as you ought to, and you will never model being a disciple of Jesus or a lover of other people as you ought to.

Sometimes, we all need to have this talk with the man or woman in the mirror: "Dude, get *over* yourself! You are not God! You are broken, flawed, and incapable of getting through the first hour of the day without an impure thought or action. But you are forgiven! In Christ you are as beloved by God, as treasured by your heavenly

Father, as you could possibly be. So get your imperfect butt out the bathroom door and share this love with other broken people, beginning with the sinners who live with you."

Model the Biblical Message in the Daily Mess of Imperfect Living

As parents, we must ask ourselves a fundamental question: When we are modeling the Christian faith for our children, which version is it? If we are (wittingly or unwittingly) modeling the "gospel of human effort," we will be found wanting by our children and all the people closest to us. We will not only reinforce the most common misconception about Christianity (that it is about following enough rules to get into heaven), but we will add an unfair burden on our kids.

One mom I interviewed put it like this: "I've been caught up for forty years in a faith that was really performance management. I don't want my kids to think that's what it means to be a Christian." This is one of the most powerful statements I've ever heard anyone make. I also notice that it is an incredibly humble, vulnerable thing to say. This is another clue, at least for me, that our power as parents is probably more connected to our vulnerability than we realize. And our vulnerability will lead us to the cross.

The Cry of the Imperfect

The following are excerpts from poetry I like to read:

> In your righteousness, rescue me and deliver me;
>   turn your ear to me and save me. (Ps. 71:2)

> Guard my life and rescue me;
>   do not let me be put to shame,
>   for I take refuge in you. (Ps. 25:20)

> Turn your ear to me,
> > come quickly to my rescue;
> be my rock of refuge,
> > a strong fortress to save me. (Ps. 31:2)

The Psalms are chock-full of such language. If I were really paying attention to what I was reading, I might ask, "What has this guy done that he always needs to be rescued? It seems as though he is in trouble all the time."

In fact, much of the material in the Psalms will make no sense to a reader who has never been in a jam, a tight space, or a deep, blue funk. There is no pretense in this poetry; in fact, the rawness of emotion we find here can sometimes offend us. The Psalms constantly reinforce the gospel drama, which is falling down, asking for forgiveness, and starting over.

If you are a parent, I recommend reading at least a psalm a day. It will help you "keep it real" and remind you that God delights in rescuing his people.

The Psalms will also help inoculate you against magical thinking—that is, the belief that there is some system, some technique, some formula which, if you only knew it, would ensure that your kids are going to turn out great. The Psalms do not present anything like a formula but rather reveal a relationship, one of God and his people.

Where We Go from Here

We've covered some ground in this chapter, beginning with the recognition of our own imperfections as parents and more generally as human beings. We've seen some very messy family dynamics in Scripture. We've also seen God work through these dysfunctional families to build his kingdom.

We've seen the connection between imperfection and community and pondered how our very imperfection might act as a guard against pride and hypocrisy.

We've considered the possibility that our imperfections might be just what God works through to do something big in our families.

One final word before we move to the next chapter, where we talk more about the home as the place where the gospel comes alive. Sometimes our imperfections cause us to live from our heels instead of our toes. Self-conscious about our shortcomings, and concerned about how we might be perceived, we approach life tentatively. We don't bring the best we have; we are not "all in" because, at some level, we are afraid. Afraid we will fail, afraid of what people will think, afraid that we will be shown for what we really are—impostors.

Beloved, if you are in Christ, you are a child of God. You have the full-on approval of the only being in the universe whose opinion actually counts. So go ahead and put both feet in—heels, toes, and all. Show up 100 percent. Bring all you have and all you are to all you do. Let that be part of your *best* will and testament to your kids.

5

Losing Control
as Your Kid Grows

Time to Develop Influence

As Lou and I were finishing our lunch, I asked how he and his wife, Kris, had navigated the transition into adulthood for each of their three kids. Here is what Lou said: "You know, Dan, I think we, as parents, know how to tell our young kids what to do, and, on the other hand, we know how to leave adult kids to their own devices, but that part in between, we are not so good at that. That's the muddy middle, and I think that is where we need to learn to ask really good questions."

In more than one focus group, parents talked about "letting out the rope" with their kids throughout the teenage years. Parents who were consciously relinquishing control while their kids were still at home seemed to be enjoying better results. They were not merely "leaving their kids to their own devices" but deliberately expanding the amount of freedom and responsibility their children had.

Here is the principle for preparing your adolescent for the college experience: parent from a place of influence, not control.

The Case for Parental Influence

Over another lunch, I was meeting with a top-notch youth and young adult pastor named Kevin. Kevin and I were discussing the disruptive nature of the transition from high school to college or full-time work. With great skill, Kevin zeroed in on root causes and potential solutions. I found myself struck, however, with what Kevin didn't talk about. Not once did Kevin mention the role of parents in the spiritual lives of their emerging adult kids. Yikes! If one of the sharpest youth workers isn't thinking about parents, the less experienced or qualified definitely are not.

I often run into parents whose thoughts mirror those of Kevin. Sometimes these parents are new to following Jesus, or they lack confidence in knowing how to model a vibrant Christian faith. More often, however, they have unwittingly bought into the cultural message that as children reach their teens their parents become invisible and inaudible. Such parents seek to hand their baton of spiritual guidance to youth experts like Kevin.

This perspective and practice contrasts sharply with the findings of sociologists like Christian Smith, the Notre Dame professor whose findings we were introduced to in chapter 1. In fact, according to Smith's research, the influence of "highly religious parents" on an adolescent is the most important of six factors that correlate with strong Christian faith in a young adult. (See sidebar "The National Study of Youth and Religion" on page 17.)

Based on a wrong assumption, parents backpedal from their involvement with their maturing kids, especially in matters of faith. Smith puts it this way:

> Oddly, this withdrawal of parental influence on adolescents seems most especially evident when it comes to religious commitments

FACTORS INFLUENCING THE FAITH OF YOUNG ADULTS

1. The influence and example of highly religious parents.
2. The high importance of religious faith for a teen.
3. The teen has many religious experiences.
4. The teen frequently prays and reads Scripture.
5. The teen has many adults in a congregation to turn to for help and support.
6. The teen has few or no doubts about religious belief.[1]

and practices. Many parents remain at least somewhat concerned to continue to exert some control over things like their children's sports prospects, educational futures, and choice of marriage partners. But when it comes to religion, many parents seem keen not to "impose" anything or to "shove religion down their throats."[2]

Here again is the quotation from *Souls in Transition* that I introduced in chapter 3:

> Thus, in the name of individual autonomy—informed here by a cultural myth that is sociologically erroneous—the usually most crucial players in teenagers' lives disengage from them precisely when they most need conversation partners to help them sort through these weighty matters.[3]

In my work with the CCO, I have encountered hundreds of thought-provoking stories and ideas about teens and faith. Even so, every time I read the quotation above, I am stopped in my tracks. Let's slow it down and look, frame by frame, at what a respected researcher is saying here.

In the name of individual autonomy. Americans have perhaps become the most individualistic people in the history of the world. We view ourselves as free agents and naturally see our kids in the same way. But this is a cultural rather than a God-created design.

Yes, we each have our own identities, distinct from any other human, but we were created to be members of communities. As humans, we are built for relationship, just as Father, Son, and Holy Spirit have always existed together in joyful love.

Too many parents buy into the notion that they have no right to interfere with their kids, particularly with their kids' beliefs. If I have to hear one more Christian parent say about their emerging adult child, "Each person has to decide what is true for himself," I may lose my lunch on someone's shoes. Human beings, including our kids, should have the opportunity to determine what they believe in the midst of a loving community, populated at least in part by people older and wiser than they are.

Informed here by a cultural myth that is sociologically erroneous. Stop the presses, people. The whole set of assumptions we currently have about teenagers may not be true! Okay, some of our assumptions are true, but when a leading sociologist says the whole "Get out of my life" thing is rooted in perception and has no real data to support it, he has my attention. Believing the myth, parents create a self-fulfilling prophecy: "The usually most crucial players in teenagers' lives disengage from them precisely when they most need conversation partners to help them sort through these weighty matters."[4] As parents, we don't think we have influence in our kids' lives, so we act as though we have no influence. *Voilà!* We now have no influence. Our teens lose us at the exact point at which they need us. We may still supply keys to the car and an allowance and help with homework, but we fail to help our kids discover the answers to the most crucial questions a human can face: Who am I? What is the meaning of life? What is my purpose?

Finally, note the phrase *conversation partners.* Smith picks words appropriate to the changing nature of the adult/child relationship as kids mature. We would not think of being a conversation partner with an eight-year-old, but as our kids grow and can express themselves more fully, conversations begin to sound more like a peer-to-peer exercise.

We cannot assume that a teen showing a bit of attitude is not paying attention. We cannot assume that our time of spiritual influence ends when our kids become teens. On the contrary, parents routinely discover years after the fact that a specific conversation or example had a lasting impact. We need to be intentional about those conversations and our example as parents.

The Scriptural Mandate

Nothing in Scripture suggests parents are done with their jobs when their children become emerging adults. In the biblical picture, family members carry responsibility for each other throughout generations.

We need to be careful not to allow the familiarity of the following passages to rob them of their power:

> Hear, O Israel: the LORD our God, the LORD is one. You shall love the LORD your God with all your heart and with all your soul and with all your might. And these words that I command you today shall be on your heart. You shall teach them diligently to your children, and shall talk of them when you sit in your house, and when you walk by the way, and when you lie down, and when you rise. (Deut. 6:4–7 ESV)

> He decreed statutes for Jacob and established the law in Israel, which he commanded our ancestors to teach their children, so the next generation would know them, even the children yet to be born, and they in turn would tell their children. Then they would put their trust in God and would not forget his deeds but would keep his commands. (Ps. 78:5–7)

The way we fulfill these roles rightly changes as our children grow, but the command to diligence does not. According to Deuteronomy 6:4–7 (above), the process starts with our own relationship with God. To be positive spiritual influencers, we must begin by loving the Lord with our whole hearts and writing his words upon our hearts. This is a tall order for anyone, and it's the prerequisite to teaching spiritual truth to our children. As the words of the Lord are written on our hearts, we have the credibility to talk about them with our kids and discover together how they connect with every aspect of life.

Our culture encourages private, innocuous, and impotent spirituality, relegated to dull Sunday mornings and the closets of our lives. Not so in the biblical picture. Deuteronomy 6:4–7 teaches us that no matter what we are doing, no matter where we are, no matter day or night, we're supposed to be talking about the Lord to our children and demonstrating how we apply his words to everyday situations.

I'm not suggesting we can make our kids believe in Jesus, particularly our teenagers—that's faulty "control" thinking. I am suggesting that the job of weaving our faith in Christ into our daily lives and conversations as parents never ends. Our challenge is to figure out how to manage this in age-appropriate and respectful ways.

I've noticed that parents who usher their kids to the front door of adulthood with a robust Christian faith are masters at moving from a more control-based mode of parenting to one of influence. Although these parents might bemoan—often playfully—their inability to tell their kids what to do and get compliance, they see the lessening of parental control as a necessary and even a good

A BEST PRACTICE

Consider a good Christian summer camp! Time away at a Christian summer camp can be a game changer. Two of our kids gave their lives to Jesus in a camp setting. Sending your child to a good camp year after year can grow him or her into a man or woman with a deeper faith. It will also provide role models to look up to and younger kids to serve.

thing. One parent explained, "I don't know when, but at some point, the relationship changes from an adult/child to more of a peer relationship."

Obviously, successfully moving from control to influence takes place on a continuum, and the earlier you build a positive relationship with your children, the better.

Mixed Messages and Awkward Transitions

Our kids have mixed feelings about our sway over them, particularly when they are growing into their own independence. We may see contrary behavior initially during the "terrible twos" and see it return many times throughout the growing-up years, particularly in adolescence. Kids often feel loving and grateful, yet angry and resentful toward their parents all at the same time. As a result, the teenager will develop the eye roll, the exasperated sigh, and the "I'm not going to look at you" posture and will use these gestures often enough that they can make us feel defeated and more than a little peeved ourselves.

The struggle toward independence and maturity is normal—and messy. For the most part, we need to take this in stride. I'm not suggesting you tolerate constant rude feedback from your kids (how can you have a safe home where people are respected when rudeness becomes customary?), but I do believe these signs of annoyance are often related to kids' naturally developing independence. A certain amount of frustration and misunderstanding is inevitable.

Remember how you felt as a preteen, early teen, and even late teen? I have what is now a strong-looking nose, but when I was fourteen, it looked like a giant handle you could use to steer my whole body. The physical changes in our kids can be a helpful reminder of changes occurring under the surface mentally, emotionally, and spiritually.

Thanks to advances in neuroscience, we now know the teenager's brain is still growing. For example, the neural pathways that help a young man determine cause and effect may not fully develop until his mid to late twenties. (Does this not explain a few things?)

There is a good side to these neural developments, which is the emergence of greater intellectual capacity, and, eventually, the ability to exercise what developmental psychologists call "executive function." Executive functioning enables us to control strong emotional and physical responses to an immediate stimulus. It is (part of) what helps a man learn to walk away from a fight or a college woman to resist unwanted pressure to have a sexual "hookup."[5]

The hard part of this churning developmental stew is that, like a stew, it looks untidy while it is cooking! As our kids manage outward physical changes, they are also dealing with the hormones involved in those changes, emotions that are strong and urgent, and intellectual thoughts they weren't capable of having before.

So if your teen is coming at life with less-than-perfect logic, it is likely part of his or her growth. Your kid is figuring it out. You may find it particularly galling that your teen doesn't seem to appreciate all you and others are doing for him or her. As is the case with rudeness, there is no reason to continue tolerating repeated ingratitude, but don't be shocked if your son or daughter is not acutely aware of the loving sacrifices you are making on his or her behalf.

Sometimes the gap in perspective between you and your child may grow unbearably intense. If they are a danger to themselves or others, look for help and consider a strong intervention. (See below, "When Intervention May Be Necessary.") Otherwise, consider the endgame, which will often require that you simply do nothing. You want to come through temporary bumps in the road with the relationship to your child still intact.

Claiming Your Circle of Influence

Steve is a Christ-follower and the dad of a college-aged child. His son, Joseph, does not participate in any Christian fellowship or church during his first year of college, partly because Steve has never asked his son to consider doing so. Although there is no guarantee that Joseph, if asked, would want to be part of a Christian fellowship on campus, his dad has never introduced the idea as a priority. This dad has given away some of his power.

Mary is a mom at a suburban church who is excited about her middle school daughter, Christina's, youth pastor. She should be; the youth pastor is an excellent leader in a great youth program. Mary, however, is assuming her role as an influential mom is now pretty much over in matters of faith. She is ceding her influence to a youth worker. Mary is giving away her power.

WHEN INTERVENTION MAY BE NECESSARY

Warning Signs

Change in routine and healthy sleep habits

Joining new group of friends who are unacceptable to parents

Recent and dramatic drop in schoolwork, attendance, or grades

Abrupt failure or refusal to contribute to the family in terms of work

Deception, lying, and keeping activities a secret

Critical Signs

Dramatic disregard for self-care and hygiene

Drugs or drug paraphernalia

Abrupt change in personality, attitude, and emotional stability

Possession of weapons

Reckless, destructive, and threatening behavior

Violent, self-harming, or suicidal statements or behavior[6]

Steve and Mary are good parents. How is it, then, that they have chosen not to use their God-given positions of influence at two crucial junctures? Chances are these parents mistakenly got caught up in an either-or concept of parenting. Once they saw themselves as appropriately releasing their right to issue directives, they felt they had to leave their kids to their own devices. They missed the strategy for the "messy middle."

All parents whose kids are in the messy middle can benefit from remembering an idea from Stephen Covey's *The 7 Habits of Highly Effective People*. Covey talks about two circles: the circle of influence and the circle of concern.[7] The circle of influence includes the people, circumstances, and things we can actually do something about—our children, our health, our work, and so on. Our circle of concern might include such things as the national debt, the weather, and terrorism. Our ability to change what is in our circle of concern is limited (though as Christians we can pray about that which is far away). Within our circle of influence, however, we always have an opportunity to shape or even just to nudge.

If we begin to think about our kids in the same way we do global terrorism or the national debt, we are in trouble. Let's consider Bob as an example of how this works in a job setting. Bob says, "I would like to bring my A game to work, but my boss is a jerk. He is at once out of touch and a micromanager."

Can you see the problem here? Bob has given his boss complete control over his working environment. Bob can neither do a great job nor enjoy his daily labor unless his boss changes. How much control do you suppose Bob has over his boss? Outside of slipping mind-altering drugs into the office coffee, not much.

Believing his boss is incompetent or, worse yet, crooked, Bob will do the minimum to get by, not believing he has the power to change anything. As the situation goes on, Bob will feel more and more powerless, which is to say that his circle of influence will shrink.

Is this beginning to sound familiar, as in the parable of the talents (or as it is called in at least one modern translation, the parable of the "bags of gold")? That's the story Jesus told where the guy thinks poorly of his boss and so he buries his coins in the ground instead of investing them like the other two guys (see Matt. 25:14–30). Not promotion material, that one.

Instead, what if Bob with the bad boss began to operate proactively (a Covey word) inside his circle of influence, building his craft and learning what matters most to his boss—sort of like the other two guys in the parable who get a nice return? Even an out-of-touch boss who micromanages appreciates a subordinate who is on top of things and makes him look good in front of *his* boss.

I've learned some hard truths about this. Every time I make an excuse ("I'm late because of traffic"), I give away power—maybe a little, maybe a lot. So if I decide this world is too toxic a place in which to raise godly children, I shrink my own circle of influence. The same thing happens if I decide my kids' peers are more influential than I am or that we have to practice on Sunday mornings if my kids are going to succeed athletically. I shrink my own circle of influence by my attitudes and behavior. It doesn't have to be this way.

We will want to be careful about allowing good sources as well as bad sources to shrink our circle of influence. I am grateful for the impact of the two wonderful men who were youth pastors to our kids, but these young men were not our kids' parents—they could not give Jack, Spence, Eliza, and Annie what Carol and I can.

The many conversations I have with Christian dads tell me that men sometimes shortchange their own influence by ceding the "spiritual head of the family" role to their wives. My wife is a strong woman—she started leading our kids to Christ at very early ages—but she can't play the role of a dad. That is my job, and the more I live into it, that is, act as a dad who is influential, the more my influence grows. This doesn't detract from Carol's influence; it creates a synergy.

In addition to the myth that parents lose all influence as kids mature, our culture offers you another dirty deal. Culture tells you to keep your faith private, confined to prayer, Bible reading, and worship. That way, nobody gets hurt. Culture bids you not to let your faith enter the public sphere where you work, play, vote, go to school, and coach.

This privatization of faith is an influence-shrinking proposition, and if we take the deal culture offers us we effectively restrict the work of God in our lives and in the world around us. Our lives lack integrity, because our faith is not integral to everything we do. Consider this paraphrase of Paul's words to the Roman church: "Take your everyday, ordinary life—your sleeping, eating, going-to-work, and walking-around life—and place it before God as an offering" (Rom. 12:1 Message).

When we live with integrity—when our faith is real and shows up on the field of play on Saturday as it will in church on Sunday— then our kids can experience the most powerful teaching tool we have: our example. If instead we have a faith that exists only in the "religious" realms of our lives, our kids are likely to be at best confused and at worst disillusioned.

Move from Control to Conversation

We have control, or something like it, early in our child's life. By the time we sit in the passenger seat of a car with our sixteen-year-old behind the wheel, things have changed. Does this mean we are relegated to merely watching as our son or daughter makes all the important driving decisions (literal and metaphorical)—right turn, left turn, slow down, speed up? Can't we at least say something if our kid crosses the double-yellow line and a head-on collision is coming our way?

When our kids are young, it is healthy to issue some directives, especially ones aimed at keeping kids safe. "Do not touch the stove; it's hot" is a directive rather than a prelude to a discussion of relative temperature, human free will, or the best way to treat burn blisters. Other reasonable directives include "Don't wrestle at the top of the stairs," "Don't play in the street," and "Do your homework."

As kids develop the capacity to understand choices and consequences, and as life becomes more complex, the commands need to turn gradually into conversations. The discussion might be on the topic of sports (the pros and cons of joining a travel team), school (why algebra is a mandatory subject), friends (how the friends we choose affect the people we become), summer jobs, or what's on television. Conversations are back-and-forth exchanges, where the child contributes his fair share of thinking and communicating. As Christian Smith says, we need to build relationships with our children as conversation partners.[8] This doesn't mean we abdicate our authority but means that we help our child move into taking more responsibility for his or her life. The degree of freedom depends on the maturity of the child and the seriousness of the issue at hand.

Eventually, a parent's best work is done by asking good questions and listening respectfully and attentively to the responses. It might go like this:

> So, you don't like our church's youth group? Tell me more about that. What bothers you most? What do you wish were different? I imagine there might be some things or people there that you like—can you list one or two? What might you do to make youth group better?

A progression unfolds as we move along a continuum from directives to conversation. The onus for considering wise, Christ-honoring ways of life transfers from parent to child. By asking questions and listening, the parent conveys respect and acknowledges, "You are not a little kid anymore." This allows the child to explore his or her own thoughts and feelings, try different options, and learn from both successes and failures, all while still under the care of loving adults. To revisit the driving analogy, our kids can practice merging onto the freeway of life while we are still in the car, rather than trying it for the first time alone. This is the stuff of healthy influence.

Depending on temperament and experience, giving up control is particularly hard for some parents. Difficult as it might be to do, giving up control in age-appropriate ways actually provides a layer of protection for your child. For example, Rosie grew up in a Christian family with a loving father who was very strict. As an adult, Rosie appreciates her dad but also recognizes the shortcomings of his approach. She reports, "As soon as I got away from home and went to college, I went crazy—partying, experimenting, and doing all the stuff I was not allowed to do at home." Her father's tight restrictions did not prepare Rosie well for the high degree of freedom she would experience in college.

This theme is familiar to CCO staff members and others engaged in college ministry. Imagine an eighteen-year-old who has always been carefully sheltered from any activity not under the auspices of his or her parents. Even at a Christian college, the range of options and the freedom to exercise those liberties will likely be more than the emerging adult can handle. Character qualities, such as self-control and the ability to delay gratification, need to develop over time. Children who have no choice but to do as their parents say right up until leaving home don't get the chance to build the life-skill muscles they will need when in college or otherwise on their own.

The process of moving from control to conversation is a stretching experience for both parents and children. Some families choose to engage in a scheduled conversation, sort of like the facts-of-life talk but without the pre-talk tremors. For example, before sending him to college, Rick Stauffer's father pulled him aside for a man-to-man talk.

"Up until now, I have pretty much told you what to do," Stauffer's dad began. "That ends today. Today, you and I become friends." These words were an acknowledgment of the change in relationship taking place under the Stauffer roof. Rick, now a father of two grown children, remembers this conversation as if it took place yesterday. It was that important to him.

A talk is a fine idea, but it doesn't always work in the way it did with Rick. As parents, we don't get to choose our moments of influence. Our children do. Our day-to-day behaviors and moment-to-moment approaches to life constitute our enduring influence. Kids often forget the *big talk*. Or vice versa. One college sophomore thanked his dad for "the talk" they had together several years before. To this day, the dad has no idea what "the talk" might have been. No, our children are more likely to remember the passing comment—one of thousands we make. In the unguarded moments of life, we teach the most. Consistency and integrity are everyday essentials.

Prioritize and Communicate Clear Expectations

In the first act of *Hamlet*, right before his son, Laertes, leaves for college, Laertes's father, Polonius, gives some advice. There is nothing wrong with the advice; in fact, we still remember "Neither a borrower nor a lender be" and other pieces of Polonius's wisdom. The problem is that Polonius dumps a whole lifetime of fatherly wisdom all at once. Shakespeare is giving a clue about how to influence productively: dispense unsolicited counsel to your kids sparingly. Moreover, make sure you have chosen the most important issues in which to meddle.

It is appropriate to communicate our expectations to our kids, particularly in the areas of life that matter most. Remember, our children acutely care about what we think. The habit of emphasizing a few important focal points, though, is critical in the years before our children leave home. You know the adage: pick the hill you are willing to die on.

As our kids go to college or enter the work world, so many matters are important. After all, our children are making decisions and choices that will set the direction for everything that follows. Both sides of the parent-kid relationship feel the pressure of choosing the right career, responsibly handling finances, finding the right mate, balancing good study habits with a good time, and protecting the young adult from real dangers. As parents love their children and want the best for them, it's natural and appropriate to communicate expectations in these areas, but it's also easy to neglect the most important matters.

Be clear about the fact that your top priority for your kids is loving and serving Jesus Christ. Talk about the fact that integrity is more important than success, and justice is more important than money.

As I mentioned earlier, Christian Smith's research shows that parents talk to their kids about faith less and less as kids move through adolescence. If we talk about careers much more than we talk about Christ, our kids are likely to get the message that careers are more important. As parents, we can unwittingly send the message that although we want our kids to be Christians, we want them to succeed in the job market even more. The danger of a mixed message is exacerbated because we fervently want life in general to be better for our kids than it has been for us. In an earlier example, we considered a parent who made a good living in a blue-collar job but still wanted his son to make a better living in a white-collar job.

Only one goal can be the top dog, and that spot needs to be reserved for loving God with our whole beings and loving our neighbors as we love ourselves. It is impossible to serve two masters. Be sure you don't send your child a mixed message about this.

Build Enduring Influence

In addition to the idea of a circle of influence, Stephen Covey introduced the idea of an emotional bank account in relationships.[9] This idea helps me understand how I can ensure that my growing child is receptive to my influence—and how I can increase the likelihood that my adult child will come to me for advice.

The emotional bank account works just like a financial bank account, with deposits and withdrawals. According to Covey (and common sense), a positive relationship depends on a positive balance. With behaviors such as courtesy, kindness, honesty, and keeping my commitments, I make deposits in any relational account. These deposits increase the trust another person extends to me.

DADS EXASPERATING KIDS

"Fathers, do not exasperate your children; instead, bring them up in the training and instruction of the Lord" (Eph. 6:4).

When we see these biblical instructions against exasperating our kids, we may think, "Aren't our kids exasperating *us*?" We exasperate as well, and Paul calls out fathers in particular. The apostle Paul could have had a number of things in mind when he instructed fathers against "exasperating" (also translated as "provoking" or "embittering") their children. On one level, there is the matter of disproportionate (unfair) discipline, which I discussed earlier in this chapter.

Exasperation, though, can come in many forms. When parents, particularly fathers, withhold their affirmation, encouragement, and affection from kids . . . well, it is enough to break your heart. It has certainly broken the heart of many a son, many a daughter. Exasperating often involves setting parameters for children's success and then manipulating the rules so that the kids are never quite good enough. Children crave their fathers' (and mothers') approval, and they assume it will come if they can just measure up. When it doesn't come, the children end up always chasing something they can't quite catch. Their ultimate reaction might resemble the words of James on the root of anger, paraphrased: "You are angry because you want something and you can't get it" (James 4:2).

This is the picture of an exasperated child: one who wants a parent's unconditional love but will never get it. If you are not a father or mother who regularly expresses love toward your kids, but withholds it (perhaps because your parent withheld it from you), break the cycle.

When others trust me, they are likely to accept my foibles and mistakes graciously.

Behaviors such as discourtesy, disrespect, cutting the other person off, overreacting, ignoring, responding in arbitrary ways, threatening, and lording it over another person all function as withdrawals. When my withdrawals exceed my deposits, the bank account is overdrawn and the relationship suffers. Trust disappears, and with it goes the grace to excuse foibles and mistakes.

Parents have to be intentional about building emotional bank accounts with their children. From the time a parent first brings a baby home to the time that parent dies, the emotional bank account is in operation. A smart parent is always building his or her reserves. Areas requiring special attention are time and discipline.

BREAKING THE CYCLE OF EXASPERATION

Carlos Sepulveda's dad and mom divorced when Carlos was seven. His dad would go on to have several more marriages and divorces while Carlos lived with his mom. His dad's interaction with Carlos during this time was very limited, sporadic, and not affirming. Carlos left his mom at age fifteen. He started working and finished high school while paying room and board to another family.

Later in life, Carlos met and married Susan, and together they brought four sons of their own into the world. Along the way, they also met Jesus Christ and learned about love, forgiveness, and God's design for their family. Here is one practice they adopted to break the cycle of exasperation that was part of Carlos's experience: virtually every night at bedtime, each Sepulveda son heard from his parents, "You're a winner, you're mine, and I love you."

That is how a parent, particularly a dad, can speak life into the hearts of his sons and daughters. You can do the same. If you need to, write something down and then say it again and again. Meaning it is key.

(Carlos Sepulveda is the former CEO of Interstate Battery and the father of former NFL punter, Daniel Sepulveda.)

Invest Time and Reap Benefits

I've always been skeptical of *quality time* where kids are concerned. I get the idea: quality time is focused, free of distraction, and in some way special. The problem is that neither toddlers nor teenagers are wired that way. Kids need *quantity time*—the more, the better, even if it means playing on the floor until your legs cramp or staying up late because that is when a teenager is ready for a conversation.

Quantity time not only helps your relational reserves, it sets the benchmark for bonding and knowing how your kids tick. If you invest time in your kids, particularly at early ages, you will have a barometer to know when you are relationally connected and when you have become distant.

Here are some ways to spend quantity time (and increase your reserves) in today's overscheduled world.

Keep potential family time, typically evenings and weekends, as free as you possibly can. With younger kids, schedule the time on your calendar in the form of activities such as walks, bike rides, zoo visits, and play dates. Develop the habit of coordinating the family calendar with your spouse regularly. With teens, you may have to schedule a parent-child day away from electronics and other distractions. Plan ahead to make this time a priority.

Adopt the "just say yes" principle. This is particularly important for parents who work outside the home. From the earliest ages, if your child wants to do something with you, say yes before you get a chance to find a reason not to. Forget how tired you are or how much you don't enjoy getting repeatedly whipped in Mario Kart. Take advantage of every opportunity to be with each of your children. Saying yes to them on their terms increases the chances they will say yes to you later.

For teenagers, "just say yes" may require creativity, because your teen is not likely begging you to do something together every week. Here are a few ideas that have worked for me:

- Zero in on something you know your child loves and see if you can spend some time together doing it. During college one of our sons and I spent a day snowshoeing together with some other folks from an outdoor club. Our daughters still enjoy going out for chocolate chip pancakes anytime I am willing. Anything your child loves can qualify as long as you are together. Trips to an art museum, a concert, or a coffee shop all qualify.

- On your birthday and at Christmas, ask for the gift of time and allow your kids to pick an activity you both enjoy. I've cashed in gifts for hikes, breakfasts, and an occasional kayak excursion.

- Look for the little stuff, hidden in plain view, such as going to the gas station together or joining forces to complete a chore.

- Enlist your child as your personal technology coach.

- Stay with it and be prepared for a few "No, thank yous" from your child.

Eat dinner (or another meal) together as often as possible. Sharing a meal with others anchors the biblical expression of community, where history culminates in the wedding feast of the Lamb. The dinner table is rightfully a place of gratitude, conversation, checking in with each other, and enjoying a meal together. Around the table, we can recall the day, open ourselves, and generally share life. The rules are simple: everybody in the family comes and contributes to the conversation, free of cell phones, television, or other distractions.

I'm not suggesting family dinners are magically positive, especially with sibling rivalry and/or sulky teenagers. Family dinners are the place where the whole family gathers. That, in and of itself, is important. In fact, researchers have correlated the practice of a regular family dinnertime to a lower risk of smoking and drinking and drug usage, better grades, and a lower incidence of both obesity and eating disorders, such as anorexia.[10] Kids whose families regularly observe the dinner ritual just generally do better in life.

If the people in your home have challenging schedules (one parent on first shift, the other on second, after-school practices or rehearsals), find the best time in the day to share a meal together. You may have to say no to some opportunities to protect family mealtime, but it will be worth the sacrifice.

Discipline with Love and Consistency

I've never felt comfortable reading the discipline sections in Christian parenting books. I've always had the impression that other parents can pick the right moment to call out their child's wrongful behavior, name it perfectly, establish exactly the right discipline, and refrain from negotiating with their child. In theory, it all seemed so straightforward.

Maybe it was because we had two sets of twins, but I wasn't always 100 percent certain which kid had done what. Sometimes, I was confused about what constituted a punishable offense and what was just highly amusing. I was capable of misdiagnosing behavior, open to negotiation (but never out-and-out bribery), and felt as if I were always making up discipline as I went. None of this fits my definition of consistency.

If you relate to these challenges, here is some good news: *consistent* and *perfect* are two very different words. Consistent discipline is marked by evenhandedness and proportionality and proves itself over time. Children on the receiving end of positive corrective action know they are loved and that boundaries in life exist for their well-being and that of others. They may get temporarily angry at the discipline, but consistent positive discipline ultimately builds a reserve rather than depletes it.

On the other hand, arbitrary or random acts of punishment erode the parent's bank account, sometimes in serious ways. A child who is grounded for a month because he or she forgets to wipe around the bathroom sink one morning will know the punishment is out of proportion. A child who is disciplined in arbitrary ways frequently will stop trusting the parent and start resisting

WHAT'S BEHIND OUR DISCIPLINE?

Here is a question that can help you discern whether you are using good, godly discipline with your kids or are—to use the verb form—"exasperating" (see Eph. 6:4) your kids by going too far. Are you setting boundaries and administering discipline to develop the character of your child, or are you doing this because you want people in your church to look at your kid and say, "He must come from a good Christian home"?

To one degree or another, your kids are a reflection of you, but they are *not* you. They will do things for reasons peculiar (sometimes really peculiar) to them and will develop in ways that neither you nor the folks in your church saw coming. It is hard not to feel proud when your kids do well and, yes, ashamed when they make bad choices or live beneath their God-given potential.

But sooner or later, you must come to grips with this: your kids do not exist to make you more emotionally fulfilled and admired. Please pay attention to that little blinking light in your brain that is activated when you begin to live your life through your kids. It is the petri dish where the virus of overcontrolling parental behavior emerges. You may not be the stage mom or that Mr. Testosterone Little League coach who embarrasses his own players, but if you are reaching for something you feel you don't have (respect, admiration, love) and trying to get it through your kids, you will do some damage, if only in the short term.

We parents should set boundaries, administer tough love, and say no to our kids. Scripture warns against raising kids in a *laissez-faire* manner, without consistent boundaries, discipline, and consequences. Yes, we spanked the little sinners in our own home, lest they would do themselves harm with their wily schemes. Appropriate structure is life-giving for kids, particularly younger ones. The words *discipline* and *disciple* do come from the same root. But parents who administer discipline in a rage or use it to shame their kids can unwittingly set traps for the children they are so desperately trying to form.

that parent's influence. Be sure your discipline is doled out for the benefit of the child rather than to satisfy your whim or anger.

The Charge

Parents who want to guide their emerging adults to the threshold of robust faith must stay involved in their child's spiritual life, even while respecting that child's right to personal decisions. Christian parents need to send a clear message that Christ comes first, even in the face of pressing demands like grades, finances, and careers. They must celebrate the wonder of God's unique design for each child, affirming strengths with consistency. Parents need to move along the continuum from control to conversation partner. Finally, they must consistently give each child the gifts of time, attention, and consistent discipline.

The good news is that parents don't lose the ability to influence their children as they become adults. I'm not saying it isn't tricky and that you won't make mistakes, but your influence is powerful, and it will last for your child's lifetime and even beyond. You can leave a legacy of love and positive influence. Take it one step at a time and trust the Lord to do the rest. You can be confident he loves your child even more than you do.

6

Center on Home

It Is Still the Place of Greatest Opportunity to Grow Faith

The whole arc of Scripture holds together with a series of covenants (serious agreements) between God and human families. God binds himself to Adam, Eve, *and their children*, to Abraham *and his offspring*, and to David *and his descendants*. Families are front and center in God's program of building a kingdom of people and making himself known throughout the earth.

From the biblical perspective, Christian parents are stewards and co-shapers with God. What an awesome and terrifying responsibility! To get the full picture of this, revisit the words from Deuteronomy we examined in chapter 5:

> Hear, O Israel: the LORD our God, the LORD is one. You shall love the LORD your God with all your heart and with all your soul and with all your might. And these words that I command you today shall be on your heart. You shall teach them diligently to your

children, and shall talk of them when you sit in your house, and when you walk by the way, and when you lie down, and when you rise. (Deut. 6:4–7 ESV)

God is interested in getting his Word under our skin, to our very core. This is the essence of having it impressed on our hearts and our souls. He wants his Word to be in front of us all the time like those sticky notes you put on your computer screen as reminders or the note on the family whiteboard to "buy more dog food!" Our relationship with his Word is to be constant, deep, and dynamic.

As we are being shaped by God's Word, we are to teach our kids. It's a process. In fact, the activity of God in our lives, formed by his words, should so penetrate us that we talk about it with our kids early, late, walking, working, eating, or worshiping. It should spill out of us.

This is the great opportunity or the great curse of family. We can rub off on each other simply because we have so much time when we are adjacent one to the other. This "principle of adjacency" allows us to be intentional in both formal opportunities (church, family worship, nightly Bible reading) and spontaneous opportunities, which often allow us to connect God's Word to daily, workweek life.

The principle of adjacency and the bonds that come with early childhood nurture mean that family experiences will "stick" with our children throughout their lives. Although they will become independent adults, our children will always, at their core, carry the model we set for them and the relationship we had with them when they were young.

Recently I attended a seminar with ten other CEOs, where we discussed our *big assumptions*, those underlying drivers that invisibly affect our everyday actions as leaders. On my left was Randall, a successful man who has grown his family business several times over. After expressing his own aspirations and fears, Randall revealed that his primary motivation is to please his father, who started the business decades earlier.

Nothing is surprising about a son wanting to please or honor his father. Randall's dad, however, has been dead for seventeen years. Yet the man's positive influence was so palpable, it was almost as if the father had pulled up a chair and joined our meeting.

Positive parental influence, as we saw in chapter 4, is not limited to perfect parents or perfect situations. You've heard unlikely stories of single parents guiding kids to successful futures against all odds. Sonya Carson, who raised two boys in an unstable home in Detroit, is one of those parents. After her marriage broke up, Sonya worked multiple jobs to make ends meet. All the while, she envisioned a brighter future for her two sons. Her standards were high, and Sonya was persistent. She also knew her sons would not thrive without God's help and the support of her church community.

Sonya Carson reports offering this prayer to God: "I don't have any friends. I don't have anyone else to turn to. God, you're going to have to be my friend, my best friend. And, you're going to have to tell me how to do things and give me wisdom, because I don't know what to do."[1] There's little doubt God answered this prayer. When Sonya didn't like a report card her son Ben brought home in fifth grade, she decided to limit him and his brother, Curtis, to two television programs per week. Instead of watching television, Ben and Curtis were expected to check out and read two books from the library each week. Just to be sure, she had the boys write book reports even though, as a woman with a third grade education, Sonya struggled to read them.

The rest of the story may be familiar to you: Sonya Carson's son Ben went on to Yale and then medical school at Johns Hopkins. In 1987, he led a team of neurosurgeons that was the first to successfully separate conjoined twins, joined at the back of the head. Carson, himself a man of faith, has gone on to perform other groundbreaking medical procedures, raise a family with his wife, Candy, write books, and rally Americans to live into their

God-given potential. Ben's brother, Curtis, also did well in life, enlisting in the military and becoming a mechanical engineer.

Stories of Randall and Ben Carson's home remind us that home is a powerful place, the most powerful place in the life of a child. Yet we look to experts in many fields—teachers, counselors, coaches, youth pastors—to do what we as parents feel we cannot do. These professionals look back at us with a clear understanding that our influence as moms and dads is exponentially greater than theirs ever can or will be.

In his discussion of spiritual gifts, the apostle Paul encourages us to look at ourselves with "sober judgment" (Rom. 12:3). In my life as a dad and leader, nothing sobers me quite as quickly as the idea that I will never have a neutral effect on another person—the effect will be either good or bad. And the closer I am to any person, the stronger our mutual influence on each other will be. (Yes, influence goes both ways, from parent to child and back again from child to parent.) As we consider how we will live in front of and beside our kids, we will want to consider with great sobriety the impact we are having.

Give Your Kids a Glimpse behind the Curtain

As researcher Brené Brown notes in her presentation *The Gifts of Imperfect Parenting*, people typically become parents somewhere about a third of the way through their lives.[2] I know that when I, fifty-five-year-old Dan, think about thirty-three-year-old Dan, I wonder how that young guy did it, because from the perspective of twenty-two years later, I know young Dan didn't know much! Yet God's design put that young Dan and his equally young wife, Carol, in charge of nurturing the next generation. How "finished" were you when God brought your children into your life?

Perhaps an important element in God's design is that we and our kids sort of grow up together—at least we travel a journey toward maturity together. The parents are ahead in the journey, but they are in no way finished learning and growing into their relationship with God. Remember the idea in Deuteronomy: as we are being shaped by God (continuous process), we are to teach our children.

Author/teacher/therapist Dan Allender remembers his own entry into parenthood this way: "What I knew about being a father could have been written several times over the head of a pin."[3] Parents are not, by definition, folks who have fully arrived, dispensing wisdom from the mountaintop to lesser beings. At one level, parents are more like "beggars showing other beggars where to find bread."[4]

In *The Gifts of Imperfect Parenting*, Dr. Brown encourages us to show our kids, as appropriate for their maturity and sense of security, the man or woman behind the curtain (think the wizard in *The Wizard of Oz* . . . my metaphor, not Dr. Brown's). The parent behind the curtain has disappointments, challenges, struggles, and failures. The parent behind the curtain is still in the process of seeking God in the midst of life.

I used to think of leadership and parenthood as processes where the parent or the leader, having achieved enlightenment and come through "many dangers, toils and snares," shares wisdom with the child or follower. Dr. Brown suggests that we consider opening our lives to our kids as we pass through these difficulties.

This is not easy for me, but it makes sense. I want our four children to see what it is like when God meets me in a hard place. They will have their own struggles in life, whether it is being fired from a job, dumped by a boyfriend or girlfriend, or dealing with their own habitual sins. If our kids have seen God meet Carol and me in our tough spots, they will know he is able and willing to walk with them through hard times.

This is the stuff of teaching our children to internalize God's promises when we sit, stand, and walk by the way—that is, when we encounter the challenges of everyday life. This is our visible response to Paul's encouragement: "Continue to work out your salvation with fear and trembling" (Phil. 2:12). The idea of a "completed parent" doesn't fit with these commands, but what does fit is our opportunity to teach from a position of vulnerability.

So consider choosing something you would just as soon not admit as a fear or a struggle and sharing it with your kids. Talk it over with your spouse first. "Mom has an opportunity for a promotion at work, but it would mean working long hours and traveling. It's the job she has always dreamt of." "Dad has been asked to do something at work that he is not sure is honest, and he isn't sure what to do." "I've been asked to make an announcement at church, but I am scared to death of talking in front of everyone."

Imagine inviting your child into a conversation about one or the other of these issues. Imagine exploring and navigating God's grace together. Imagine this model being an enduring influence in the entire life of your child.

Here is another way to look at it: experts do not necessarily make the best teachers. We often teach well what we ourselves are still learning. As the leader of a growing campus ministry, I am learning how to be less involved in the day-to-day operations of the CCO and focus on a different set of issues. The process is fresh right now, and since large parts of it don't come naturally, I'm conscious of each step. This struggle, rather than any expertise, puts me in a good position to share what I'm learning with the next generation of leaders.

As a leader in your family, you may be learning, really learning, for the first time, how to pray. It is not natural to you; you need to think about it. You are in a perfect position to share this with your kids, whether it is as simple as "Close your eyes and start talking to God," or "Here is the outline I use: Adoration, Confession, Thanksgiving, Supplication (ACTS)," or "Let's memorize the Lord's Prayer together."

Celebrate Your Children's Gifts, Not Their Gaps

Carol and I did not know if we were ever going to be parents. Eight years into our marriage, we had long since borne the official label, *infertile*. When the day finally came to deliver twins by C-section, I was warned to get some breakfast. "We will have two of everyone in the delivery room. We don't need you to make things interesting by passing out."

Two mostly red, scrunchy-looking, beautiful baby boys emerged. The birth announcement was funny (to us anyway), with the image of the Macaulay Culkin open-mouthed, hands-on-cheeks scream, announcing that we were no longer *Home Alone*. Inside, the announcement expressed both the pain of infertility and the joy of having our first kids: "You have turned our mourning into dancing"

WHEN OUR KIDS BECOME THANKFUL FOR US

Sometimes teenagers are able to tell us about our influence on them when they are still in middle or high school, but I would not recommend expecting this to happen. You might be disappointed! Later, though, during the college years and beyond, young people are able to articulate a sense of deep, moving gratitude for their parents. Here are two examples from my research:

From a college junior to her parents: "You guys always really encouraged us to be independent in our prayer lives—like if we were dealing with a problem you would ask us if we prayed about it. But you also did this through example, when you would get up in the morning and do your devotionals—that was a model we learned to follow—children really learn through modeling and repeating so this made a big difference!"

From a twenty-five-year-old daughter: "Probably the most important thing my parents did that influenced me the most was that they lived out their faith first and foremost. It would be easy for them to discipline us, tell us what they expected from us but then turn around and do whatever they wanted. Kids aren't dumb, they pick up on these things very quickly. I saw both my parents in the Word daily, they never forced that on us, yet they demonstrated what Christian living looked like."

(see Ps. 30:11). We felt the same way four years later when our twin girls were born.

One of the greatest gifts parents can give a child is to maintain the sense of wonder they feel at that child's birth. Parents do their job best (and enjoy it most) when they consider themselves explorers, seeking to discover and affirm the unique person God designed each child to be. When a parent treats a child's unique design as a wonder, that child grows in both emotional and spiritual health.

In the crush of everyday life, however, many of us fall into *deficit parenting*. In other words, we focus on shortcomings and weaknesses. Rather than helping our children develop their God-given strengths, we push them to get better in areas outside their gifts. It makes sense to ask our kids to become *competent* in all functional areas of life, but it goes against God's design to push them to *excel* where they are not gifted. Driving our kids in this way can make them feel inadequate rather than affirmed.

In his book, *StrengthsFinder 2.0*, Tom Rath describes his work with a team of Gallup scientists led by the late Donald Clifton. Here's what Rath says:

> We were tired of living in a world that revolved around fixing our weaknesses. Society's relentless focus on people's shortcomings had turned into a global obsession. What's more, we had discovered that people have several times more potential for growth when they invest energy in developing their strengths instead of correcting their deficiencies.[5]

Beginning work on identifying strengths forty years ago, Gallup has surveyed more than ten million people worldwide on the topic of employee engagement. This research shows that people who have the opportunity to focus on their strengths each day at work are "six times as likely to be engaged in their jobs and more than three times as likely to report having an excellent quality of life in general."[6]

Strength-based coaching has become a widespread practice among business coaches and leaders. I use it in my leadership at the CCO, and I believe focusing on strengths more than weaknesses has helped us to be recognized consistently as one of the best Christian places to work in the United States.[7] It seems crazy, however, to wait until our kids enter the work world to identify and celebrate their strengths. If God, the Creator, is the author of all strengths, we need to be discovering and encouraging those strengths in the context of our homes, beginning when our children are very young. And we need to be giving God the credit. He is the one, after all, who assigns different members of the body their particular gifts (and loves watching us use them!).

Even when their children are at the youngest ages, parents can notice and affirm natural talents. This is co-shaping with God. Recently, three small children visited our home. The three-year-old was drawn to her baby sister and genuinely enjoyed her part in feeding, diapering, and playing with her. The five-year-old went for the art supplies and started in, nearly oblivious to the existence of his siblings.

To the mother of these three, this was not a one-time phenomenon. The three-year-old seems hardwired to help, particularly with a younger sibling, and the five-year-old will gravitate to any available artistic medium. Carol and I listened as the children's mother caught them in the act of using their gifts: "Wow. God designed you with the heart of a helper. You are good at it." "God has given you a love to create beautiful things. How great is that?!"

Appreciation for the expression of a child's interests and gifts helps build confidence and a better relationship between parent and child. Talking about God-given gifts throughout childhood prepares a child to begin discerning his or her vocational direction.

Parents can also affirm their children's emerging character strengths. In the day to day, it might sound like this:

Erin, it's great that you decided to try out for the track team. One of the things I admire about you is your willingness to try new things, even if you have little or no experience with them. This willingness shows courage and the integrity to follow through on stuff you think of. Tell me more about running track. What part is most exciting and interesting to you?

It might be difficult to talk like this to your child at first, especially if your parents didn't offer much by way of verbal affirmation. Noticing what others do well and affirming them for it is like using a muscle. It may take a while to get conditioned if you have not been using that muscle much. No matter how awkward you feel at first, do not back off or give up on the habit of affirming your kid's strengths. Make yourself accountable with another mom or dad. We meet too many kids on college campuses who arrive starved for the affirmation and approval of their parents.

As kids approach their teen years, strengths-based tools are available to help them gain greater clarity as to how God has designed them. The Gallup organization has readily accessible tools for discovering strengths and engaging in discussions about them with your teens. Rath's book, *StrengthsFinders 2.0*, guides the reader to discover his or her unique strengths among thirty-four themes. It also guides the reader to practical ways to apply those strengths.

Such tools can help both parent and child to be on the lookout for particular expressions of how God uniquely made each of them. This knowledge not only serves as affirmation and a guide to the child, it helps the parent avoid the trap of trying to mold the child into his or her image. Knowing our child's gifts helps us rediscover the wonder we felt at his or her birth.

You might be skeptical about this approach and asking, "Isn't it part of my job as a parent to teach my kids accountability—that they have to live up to their responsibilities even if that means struggling through things for which they do not have a natural talent?"

JIM AND KATE

To say Jim was ambivalent about dropping his oldest daughter off at the state university campus in Ohio would be an understatement. Kate was enrolling in a tough program—architecture—but that didn't have him worried. What did worry him was this: as if they couldn't wait for the parents to make the drop-off and get on their way, the men on fraternity row were firing up the party machine, carrying beer into their houses, cranking up the music, and hanging suggestive signs just in case they hadn't put down enough clues already.

At the same time, Jim was wondering about the other influences on campus. He was aware that the environment Kate was headed into wasn't going to be faith-friendly. From his perspective, the entire higher education edifice was going to bring a significantly different view of life to his daughter, and possibly do it aggressively. So with temptation to dissipation on one side of the street, and the hostile ideological underpinnings of the university on the other, two things were abundantly clear: he was leaving his daughter in a vulnerable (possibly dangerous) place, and he was writing the school a big check for the privilege!

This story taps into the parental fear I have heard cataloged for years, reflecting what we at the CCO have heard in response to this question: "What are your top concerns about college students and the college experience?" Once the honest discussion begins, we hear plenty in the parental anxiety closet, but the most frequent responses from Christian parents are similar to the questions Kate's father is essentially asking: "Will my child succumb to the lifestyle temptations college presents and make choices that will permanently alter her life? Will she drink away her common sense or fully join the 'hookup' culture of casual sex? Will she decide her faith is not intellectually defensible and fold like a lawn chair at the first confrontation with a competing view of life?"

Even with all the temptations to party or to work hard and neglect her faith, Kate made it through. She is gainfully employed as an architect, owns her faith, and is committed to Christ's work in the world. Kate had seen what faith looked like in her own home and had a rich network of Christian friendships even before college. By her own admission, she did not do everything right during her college years—she tried some of the partying and went long stretches without attending church. But she had a healthy "default setting"; that is, she knew what it meant to be in fellowship with God and with other believers. That was what she wanted and ultimately what she pursued.

Yes, your kids do need to learn how to do what they are expected to do, whether or not it comes easily. As parents, we guide them to answer this question: "Given who you are, how are you going to get this done?" The assumption is that the child will work that math problem to completion, finish that English paper, or learn that song. Repeatedly letting your kids off the hook is bad for their development. Part of our work is to help them figure out how to fulfill their responsibilities given who they are. Teaching children responsibility need not conflict with affirming their unique design.

Practical Suggestions to Make Your Home a Place of Positive Influence

Married or single, make the culture of your home your first priority. A loving home is the best gift we can give to our kids. Our children know when things are good between Mom and Dad and are much more perceptive than we realize when things are bad. A tense, fractious home environment negatively affects kids, particularly when the result is divorce. No experts dispute this, be they social researcher, therapist, or pastor. How do we end up with something other than the best marriage we can build together? And how do we give our kids what they need in a solo-parent home?

The paradox of raising children is that they are at once the greatest joy in a marriage and the greatest source of stress on the marriage. Kids need what they need *now*, whereas your mate is capable of waiting. Most moms are hardwired to deal with the needs of their children first, their spouse second. Men whose wives respond to their children that way often reciprocate by becoming distant from their wives, pursuing their well-being elsewhere, oftentimes at work.

If you are married, building a great marriage is the best gift you can give your children. Consider the following suggestions for strengthening your marriage:

- Have a regular date night, weekly if possible. Remember that, as a lover and influencer, time is your most precious asset. Sit down regularly with your spouse and your calendars. Bring your calendars to your date night and arrange schedules for the next week. Every three months or so, look ahead through the next half or whole year. This will help you hash through your highest priorities as a family, which will lower the amount of conflict you have with your husband or wife. You will also have a much higher likelihood of doing what you think is important as a family.

- Join a small group in your church. To make marriage work, you need supportive relationships from men and women other than your spouse.

- If you are in a season of trouble (unresolved conflict, a sense of "drifting apart," a lack of sexual intimacy), meet with your pastor or a Christian counselor and ask for help. The short-term discomfort of working through things together is preferable to the long-term pain of a dying marriage.

If you are parenting alone, God is at work in your home too. He is the God of people who are in tight spots, and he delights in rescuing us when we are at the end of our resources. As a married individual, I am reluctant to give advice about this, but I know good resources are available, particularly through websites such as *Today's Christian Woman* and *Focus on the Family*. Resources such as divorce recovery groups are also likely to be available through your church or another church nearby.

I do recall the words of Angela Thomas, a single mom of four, as she learned to walk with God through life after a divorce: "I came to find that I set the tone of my home. I'm it."[8]

Single mothers Sonya Carson, Angela Thomas, and a number of single fathers I've talked to have learned they have the ability to shape the environment in their homes. Although the sense of powerlessness that often accompanies the death of a spouse or a divorce can be overwhelming, solo moms and single dads can build a healthy home for their kids.

Model spiritual disciplines. The best way to encourage your kids to have regular time alone with God is to have it yourself. Find a way to spend time with God that works for you. You may not be that morning person who has already prayed for two hours when everyone else gets up. Evening may work a whole lot better. Some families have regular times of worship around the dinner table, and some don't. As you are considering the relationship of your children to God, make your own growth and the habits that support that growth the highest priority.

Speak your faith. This is the flip side of a myth we visited in chapter 3, "Saying it is enough." When it comes to passing the baton of faith, your example is enormously important, but it is not enough. Take some risks to talk about your walk with God. If that is hard for you to do, ask this question at the dinner table: "What was one thing that happened today for which you are thankful to God?" Share yourself, beginning with the phrase, "I'm thankful to God for. . . ." Just ahead in this chapter are some gratitude practices that will prime the pump for a good dinnertime conversation.

As appropriate, share moments when following God is hard.

Most of all, take advantage of the opportunity to pray with your kids. We kept this simple at our house. Every night the boys and I prayed for one thing for which we were thankful, and we offered one request to God. I remember how, early in the Rwandan civil war, Jack, Spence, and I would ask God to help the Hutus and the Tutsis (the tribal groups in conflict) stop killing each other. This journey of prayer together linked us to brothers and sisters far away from Pittsburgh.

Follow a healthy practice for dealing with conflict. The practice of giving and receiving forgiveness is as important as anything we teach our children. Each time one confesses and another forgives, we are involved in a gospel mini-drama, where we aren't just talking about the gospel but living it.

We've said the words in the Lord's Prayer so often that we've become numb to them, but allow this part of Jesus's model of prayer to sit with you for a moment: "Forgive us our debts [sins], as we have forgiven our debtors [those who have sinned against us]" (Matt. 6:12). It's hard to get around what follows: "For if you forgive other people when they sin against you, your heavenly Father will also forgive you. But if you do not forgive others their sins, your Father will not forgive your sins" (Matt. 6:14–15). There is a sense in which our forgiveness from God is contingent on or proportional to our forgiveness of others who have sinned against us. Christians are forgiven of an enormous debt by God. Forgiving others is not optional for us. How much easier will it be for our kids to forgive if we teach them from the earliest age how it works?

Confession and forgiveness between parent and child might sound something like this (not that anything remotely like this ever happened in our family):

> "John, I am sorry I made you feel really, really bad when you struck out in your Little League game. Baseball is supposed to be fun, but I made it un-fun by criticizing you when you didn't swing your bat on the third strike. I was wrong. Will you forgive me?"
>
> "Dad, I wish you hadn't done that. But I forgive you."

Notice the two primary parts to the process: a confession that names the sin (or what you understand the sin to be) and the words, "I forgive you." Regarding confession, it is important to admit wrong, rather than sugarcoat your mess with the now-popular term, "I made a mistake." Harassing a ten-year-old for striking out is not a mistake; it is an offense, a wrong.

Encourage the offended party to refrain from saying, "That's okay," which is often used to end an uncomfortable conversation. The selfish or mean behavior is not okay. It wounds and offends. The words "I forgive you" acknowledge the offense and the pain, and they bring the wounded and the culprit right to the gospel. We learn to forgive because we have ourselves been forgiven. In

99

Christ, God has separated our sin from us "as far as the east is from the west" (Ps. 103:12).

Use words to build up, not to tear down. Children in every age have found ways to artfully craft language in a way that puts a brother, sister, or peer in his or her place. In my youth, calling someone a "fathead" was one way to get this done. Our friends the Towners, realizing the corrosive power of words, discouraged the use of "fathead," "doofus," or any number of creative monikers their sons Ric and Russ brought home from school or the neighborhood. On one occasion when Russ was caught calling Ric a fathead, he responded, "But Mom, he really does have a fat head!"

The degree to which human beings will use language to wound others should not be underestimated. The Bible, more than any book I've ever read, seems most realistic about two painful realities:

1. Humans can be nasty pieces of work. We are created in God's image, true, but in our fallen state, we can be like a giant barn, filled to the hayloft with manure.

2. The impact of words spoken from the "manure barn" is powerful enough to destroy another person.

It is for these reasons that the writer of Proverbs draws our attention to what we say: "The tongue has the power of life and death, and those who love it will eat its fruit" (Prov. 18:21).

Jesus masterfully turns a conversation about keeping kosher to a summary of a much bigger problem: "What goes into someone's mouth does not defile them, but what comes out of their mouth, that is what defiles them" (Matt. 15:11).

Letters in the New Testament frequently cite the kind of talk that is appropriate for Christians, particularly with each other. James says it most forcefully: "All kinds of animals, birds, reptiles and sea creatures are being tamed and have been tamed by mankind, but no human being can tame the tongue. It is a restless evil, full of deadly poison" (James 3:7–8).

The inverse of killing with the tongue is using it to give life by encouraging each other (see 1 Thess. 5:11; Heb. 3:13), using gentle speech (see Col. 4:6; Prov. 15:1–2), and speaking the truth in love (see Eph. 4:15).

The starting place is once again your example. How do you talk to your kids when you are disappointed or angry? How do you talk about people who are not in the room? When you don't feel so great about yourself, do you use putdowns of others (subtle or "fathead") to feel better about yourself? Are you using some of the same hurtful language with your kids that you heard from one of your parents when you were young?

Because the tongue is such a dangerous weapon, you will probably have to talk to your kids about their use of words from time to time. Carol had this question ready for such occasions in our home: "Are you trying to make your brother [or sister] feel better?"

Show hospitality. Chocolate truffles, Honeycrisp apples, and a bottle of water by each of our beds. That's the kind of hospitality our friends the Walkers extend whenever we visit them at their home in New Jersey. The snacks are one way Bill and Debbie make it clear that you are not only welcome, but that they are delighted to have you stay with them.

You may or may not have the gift of hospitality. Either way, it is good for your kids to see you invite others into your home and treat your guests with honor and affection. This is a golden rule moment that takes place in your own kitchen. In our culture, particularly in this day and age, we have relegated hospitality and its highest expressions—the sharing of a meal—to the back burner. If you are privileged to experience another culture, either here or out of the country, you will likely experience the honor of being a guest and the ritual of a real, shared meal.

The encouragement to be hospitable in Scripture is both a reference to the actual experience of Abraham and Sarah and an appeal to our imaginations: "Do not forget to show hospitality to strangers, for by so doing some people have shown hospitality to angels without knowing it" (Heb. 13:2).

Develop compassion. "I remember my mother giving food to the hobos who stopped by our back door. They were men who had lost their jobs and their dignity and were drifting from town to town, dirty and skin and bones." This is a Depression Era memory of a friend that stuck with her through the rest of her life.

Compassion for others can be planned (helping in a soup kitchen, sponsoring a child through Compassion International or World Vision) or serendipitous (helping a man in a wheelchair open a heavy door). Our friends the Dalys spend a week every year as a family with Joni and Friends, serving parents whose children are severely disabled and need constant care. Most of us have everyday opportunities to model uncommon courtesies (opening doors for others, not eating until everyone is served, saying "thank you") that help our children understand the value of other human beings.

A current discussion in the church and elsewhere probes what is true compassion versus unhealthy enabling. My office is in a neighborhood where I might regularly be asked for money to "buy food" or "catch a bus." The counsel we received early on from a local compassion ministry was to look the person in the eye and say gently, but firmly, "Sorry, man, but I can't." The chances are very high that the money we would give in such circumstances would go toward drugs or alcohol, not food. I've taken a person or two to McDonald's for breakfast, but no longer give out cash.

When you are engaged in acts of compassion with your children, consider the issue of human dignity. When we do something for someone they can do for themselves, we may rob them of dignity. People accrue dignity when they can be engaged in meaningful work, and at least to some degree, support themselves and their families. To the degree that it is possible, tilt your acts of charity to causes that are trying to help others find their own way. One option is to engage in micro-financing opportunities, with small loans to help launch enterprises in the developing world. Hope International, World Vision, and Kiva are all reputable nonprofits that connect giving people with micro-finance needs. Which brings us to the delicate topic of money.

Address money. Scripture talks more about money than just about any other topic, save God himself. It is a big deal as evidenced by Jesus's words, "Where your treasure is, there your heart will be also" (Matt. 6:21). You, like me, may not feel adequately equipped to teach your kids the ABCs of Christian financial literacy, but great resources are available to help kids understand how to think about and use money in a God-honoring way. Good $ense Ministry, for example, has a video-based curriculum called *Raising Financially Freed-Up Kids.*

In many of our families, money was never talked about. While you may not want to show your kids your monthly pay stub (or maybe you do . . . your choice), you should involve them in giving and other financial decisions whenever you can.

I am intimately familiar with one part of this topic: giving. Half of my job leading the CCO has been raising money. The best gift you can give your child with regard to money, in my opinion, is modeling how to liberally give it away. If you don't come from a family where tithing (giving away 10 percent of income) was practiced, start working toward that 10 percent. Ten percent is the starting place—I've known couples who give away more than 50 percent of their annual income. Enroll in a workshop at your church or another that will help you move toward generosity with your finances.

Learning to "hold loosely" the money God provides and giving generously are the best antidotes I know to protect against covetousness (Old Testament commandment No. 10) and greed, "which is idolatry" (Col. 3:5). Through all these years of watching as men and women made aggressive giving decisions, I have seen the joy and wonder they experience as God provides in unexpected ways. Carol and I have found it to be true that "you can't out-give God."

Practice gratitude. The good use of money, and giving in particular, are both rooted in the same discipline: gratitude. You may have thought of gratitude as more of an emotion or disposition ("attitude of gratitude") and may be surprised to see it called a "discipline," but I believe it is. Like other disciplines, it is a practice we choose to bring ourselves under, and it is a habit that gets better and easier as we do it more.

Here is what I've learned about gratitude: it doesn't count unless you express it to someone. My pastor, Dan Hendley, makes the distinction between "thanks-feeling" and "thanks-giving." Thanks-feeling is unexpressed gratitude, which comes across our emotional radar, usually for a brief moment, and then goes away.

Thanks-giving takes that momentary feeling of warmth and expresses it to God or to another person. The gratitude loop is not complete until we tell someone—preferably the one to whom we should be thankful. At that point, gratefulness passes from a fleeting feeling to a permanent pin-drop in our souls. We also bless the recipient of our thanks-giving, whether that is God or another person.

So how do we stoke the fires of gratitude in ourselves and in our children? Here are two ideas:

- Keep some kind of "gratitude journal." Doctors and others have observed the emotional and physical health benefits of expressing thanks. Don't overthink this.

  Option A: At day's end, think through the day and write down everything you can recall for which you can be thankful. Don't worry if it seems small; in fact, go after the small, seemingly insignificant stuff. "They had pumpkin soup in the cafeteria. I love pumpkin soup!"

  Option B: You can also begin each day with a similar exercise, but this time zero in on the question, "To whom do I want to express gratitude today?" This lays the groundwork to move from thanks-feeling to thanks-giving.

- Every time you go on an adventure as a family, whether it's camping overnight, visiting grandparents, or a full-blown vacation, have a "thank-fest." The rules are simple: everyone thinks about each part of the adventure and blurts out something for which they are thankful. We are looking for quantity here, and no judging of other people's favorite moments is allowed. Among the six of us, we've come up with one hundred "thanks things" on our list after certain vacations. Sitting around the dinner table and doing this is also a bit like living the adventure all over again. I've kept each of these lists in my journals, and they go back seventeen years.

The practice of thanks-giving primes the pump for joy so big and so wonderful, you may consider it beyond your grasp. But joy is the birthright of the Christian.

Develop joy. Who are the most joyous people you know? What's interesting to me is that those who practice joy do so in circumstances that don't seem to support the idea of human happiness. Years ago the CCO lost one of our best, Michael Barbato, to melanoma. Michael and Kristi were in their early thirties and had two little boys. It was a long and difficult struggle, ultimately ending in Michael's death. When I would see Michael, I felt as if he was ministering to me, not the other way around. He had an authentic *joie de vivre* (joy of life) about him, whether feeling well enough to reach out to college students or suffering through the worst of cancer.

When our daughter Annie spent a week helping lead Vacation Bible School at two Haitian orphanages, she was caught off guard by the joy of people who had little to celebrate by worldly standards. It makes one wonder if there might not be an inverse relationship between the stuff we have, which we always think makes us happier, and the experience of real joy, which depends neither on circumstances nor on material possessions.

The Scriptures are rather insistent that we learn the practice of joy. "Rejoice in the Lord always. I will say it again: Rejoice!" (Phil. 4:4). "For the kingdom of God is not a matter of eating and drinking, but of righteousness, peace and joy in the Holy Spirit" (Rom. 14:17).

I wish I had some "easy steps to joy" to recommend so you might model this fruit of the Spirit in your home. It doesn't seem to work that way. Like real fruit, we cannot produce the fruit of the Spirit by sheer human effort ("Grow already, little green apple"). It is cultivated in the human heart by the Holy Spirit. Our job is to cooperate, to make our hearts and minds soft landing places for everything we can learn about God and about gratitude.

For now it is enough to ask, "How am I modeling joy in front of my kids? How would I like to be modeling joy?"

The Charge

You may have a white picket fence around your yard or live in a tiny third-story walkup. You may vacation in Hawaii or at a state park in a tent. Your marriage may be ideal, it may be rocky, it may be nonexistent. Whatever your situation, if you are a parent, your home is your domain. It is a place of great responsibility and of great power. It is the place that will shape your child like none other. And with God's help, you can shape it to be a great place for your kids.

So decide to take a small step today to make your home a more Christ-centered place. Pick one thing you will stop doing. Then pick one thing you will start doing. If you occasionally fail, ask forgiveness, get up, and try it again. Pray. Enlist the help of others. Remember, this is big. This matters. Don't give up, no matter what. Watch for God to do something.

When you think about your influence and/or failure to be intentional, do not despair. The Holy Spirit is not finished.

7

Invite Community

Good Parenting
Requires More Than Parents

During a free speech rally at UC-Berkeley in 1964, activist Jack Weinberg famously said, "Don't trust anyone over thirty."[1] Countless young people made this their credo. By now, however, Weinberg and his peers have long since passed thirty, as have their children. Presumably, none of them are to be trusted!

At least since the 1960s, we've come to believe that all teenagers have adopted Weinberg's credo—hook, line, and sinker. We have cultivated a myth that teenagers respond to the influences of their peers, their favorite media (entertainers, athletes, games), and maybe their very cool youth pastors—but never to grownups, those graying, overweight adults who wear embarrassingly uncool clothes, are hopelessly out of touch, and cannot find any point of connection with kids. In fact, we adults believe ourselves to be impotent and even largely invisible to the teenagers who float through our space.

Even if you don't completely buy into the view that teenagers find all adults irrelevant, you might be surprised about where the research regarding today's youth points. The data, particularly from the National Study of Youth and Religion (NSYR), suggests that young people want, even long for, the influence of caring adults in their lives. In fact, *the influence of caring Christian adults* is among the six factors from the NSYR that correlate to a successful faith transition during college.

The big surprise is that the help and support of other Christian adults shows up right where we might expect to see peer influence (or some other more obvious item, like mission trips). What's more, the support of Christian adults comes from individuals in the emerging adult's congregation. Even the less-than-cool church people who show an interest in your child's life turn out to be a big deal. A very big deal. And the less-than-cool *you* can make a difference in the lives of other kids besides your own. In fact, these other kids *need* you.

Introverted and Wounded Friends, Relax

In this chapter and the next, I'll be making a case for opening your life and home to other adults and kids. I'll be advocating for both hospitality and some vulnerability. If you are introverted or have experienced a deep wound from a friend, please read both chapters, which are integrated, with an open mind.

The Bible, for the most part, addresses a community rather than individuals. It *assumes* we will be in fellowship with others outside of our immediate family. Community is the route to the positive adult influences your child needs to mature. For it to work, the fellowship has to have some consistency and some depth.

Fortunately, the Bible doesn't tell us everyone, even those who are introverted, needs to hang out in large crowds or that any of us must make ourselves vulnerable to others who are untrustworthy. With prayer, God will help each family work out community in its own way.

How Positive Adult Influence Works

Adult influence can't be easily programmed, particularly for teenagers. If you want other Christians to speak into the life of your child, you must create a context where this can happen. Our kids will benefit from the influence of other believing adults most readily when we are in consistent, deep relationships with other Christ-following grown-ups.

Christian families who raise their children in relative isolation will lack access to one of the six influences that boosts their kids' likelihood to become faithful followers of Jesus. Our kids need other adults who demonstrate not only how to negotiate what it means to be *in* the world without being *of* the world, but also how to be salt and light where they live. Strong families are the starting point, but not the ending point. The ending point is the body of Christ, since "from him the whole body, joined and held together by every supporting ligament, grows and builds itself up in love, as each part does its work" (Eph. 4:16). Your kids need to see that other respectable grown-ups are as crazy about Jesus as their parents.

As a parent, you need other believing adults to be strong where you are weak. Perhaps the family in which you grew up was not so great. Perhaps you never had the benefit of watching how loving parents interact with each other and their kids. You are improvising with little feel for what you are doing. You and your kids would benefit from friendships with other Christians who had the gift (quite unearned) of a healthy family, anchored by loving parents, both father and mother.

Your kids need models of healthy families and diverse individuals. They need other believing adults to connect with them in ways you cannot. For example, you might be an engineer raising an aspiring painter, or two artsy people entrusted with the nurture of an emerging business dynamo. Other believing parents with differing careers and temperaments can help.

It lends power and credibility to the gospel message when your children see it embraced by people for whom they have affection and respect and who they know are genuinely interested not only in Jesus but in them.

Sarah Walko, whom you will read more about later, and Darrell Throckmorton were born at the same hospital on the same day. Their parents, who attended the same church, became fast friends, and the kids followed suit. These two families formed a sort of nuclear core that drew in other families and built a web of relationships so firm that all the parents had the green light to act on each other's behalf in matters of discipline with visiting children.

Not only did kids from these families show up at one another's homes, but the families also got together, often just to have fun. Parents and kids formed bonds across family lines because they spent time together.

As several other families gathered around the Walko and Throckmorton core, kids came to understand that they had, in their language, "a second set of parents." That is, they had adults other than their parents to talk to in a time of need. The children from these families are now young adults, but they still avail themselves of a sit-down with a "second mom" or "second dad" when life throws a curve ball and they need a listening ear.

In the mid 1980s, Carol and I, together with a few of our twenty-something friends, started a small group. Over time, we had kids and bought houses. Some of us eventually took jobs out of town, but, on the whole, we have stayed in touch.

Four families, with fourteen kids among us, have kept a particularly close connection over the years and across the miles, even as kids have gone to college, found jobs, and met future spouses. Only recently did the youngest ones learn they are not actually related!

The result is a bond built between kids and adults that functions like a clear highway where influence can freely travel. The bond is priceless for the kids and also for the adults.

Imagine other contexts, like the following, where trusted adults can "do life" alongside your kids:

- Over the summer, a local church sent fifty teens and eight adults on a one-week mission trip. Of the adults, only two currently had teenage children. Two couples, each with grown kids of their own, each took a week of vacation to spend it with fifty teenagers. They were joined by a father of three small boys and an eighty-year-old grandfather.

- Acts of service generally lend themselves to generation-mixing. It is good to visit older people in a nursing home, but it is much better if young people go along.

- In some churches, parents help form and lead small groups for kids who are part of the church youth group. These groups can be an official part of the youth ministry program, but they can also be initiated more informally. Regular contact brings the opportunity for influential relationships.

- Family camps are frequently available at Christian campsites. These camps allow kids and adults to flow freely in and out of each other's worlds. The amount of potential influence in these settings is limitless.

- Christian adults who become coaches, scoutmasters, and Sunday school teachers build important relationships with the kids in their care. I have a friend who takes kids and dads on a yearly cross-country ski expedition in the White Mountains.

- Old-fashioned church potluck dinners, where everyone brings a dish to share and enjoy, create opportunities to build relationships.

These are all examples of ways to fulfill God's call to relationship, expressed with great power across generations throughout Scripture.

The Call of Scripture: "One-Anothering"

Scripture is written not so much to individuals as it is to a people, a community of faith. Therefore, we should not be surprised to find no fewer than fifty-nine New Testament directives on how to "one another" each other. "Love one another . . . accept one another . . . forgive one another . . . bear one another's burdens. . . ." These "one-another" principles are meant to apply across the whole body of Christ, including those younger than we are. Just because kids can't reciprocate, particularly when they are little, doesn't mean we don't have obligations to treat them as fellow members of our faith community. What would it look like to put some "one-anothering" passages to work in our relationships with young children and teenagers outside our immediate family?

CHURCH: PLEASE EMBRACE A COLLEGE STUDENT

Most Christian parents I've interviewed over the years do not expect their kids to show up in church every Sunday when they go off to school. Truth be told, parents are pretty well ready to let go of the church idea altogether. How can we expect our sons and daughters to get up on a Sunday morning after a busy week of studying and partying? This is one of the myths I addressed in chapter 3, but it bears repeating because church provides a college student with ongoing exposure to caring Christian adults.

Many parents believe college Christian fellowships are a suitable stand-in for church during college. As chairman of the board of the CCO, I'm grateful for CCO-led fellowships on 115 campuses. These fellowships are awesome, but they are not church. Only church provides the intersection of Christian community where adults love and mentor youth and where youth learn to worship, serve, and lead.

Back in chapter 3, I gave you two examples of churches who reach college students. Plenty of other churches do as well. Like the Christ Community in the South Hills/Point Park University example earlier, Gateway Church in Findlay, Ohio, is four miles from the University of Findlay campus. Still, about forty students find their way to church, which is a CCO partner,

Throughout Scripture, adults nurture other people's offspring. Although the high priest Eli isn't so great at raising his own kids, he seems to do right by Samuel, the young prophet-in-training entrusted to him. Fast-forward to the New Testament and you see more nonparental, caring adults. Consider Barnabas, one of Paul's ministry partners. In fact, Barnabas refuses to leave a young pastor-in-training, John Mark, behind to travel with Paul. John Mark has let Paul down before, and Paul doesn't believe the young man should go on the next missionary journey. Paul and Barnabas disagree so strongly on this that they agree to part ways. I'm not suggesting that Paul acts inappropriately; I'm pointing out Barnabas's faithfulness to his young charge (see Acts 15:36–41).

Paul has several younger protégés, most notably Timothy, who

every week. Gateway rents a house across the street from the university and hosts about sixty-five collegians for dinner every week—more evidence that if you feed them, they will come.

Brookdale Community Church partners with the CCO to reach commuter students at Brookdale Community College, a school in mid-state New Jersey. The church recently added a discipleship house for college students. Bellefield Presbyterian Church is surrounded by the University of Pittsburgh, whose students flock to the church on Sundays and for the Bellefield–CCO weekly fellowship, Cornerstone. This is another forty-year-plus partnership.

As much as I love campus Christian fellowships—your child should absolutely be in one—I know they cannot take the place of the church, where not everyone is between eighteen and twenty-two and really cool. Church is where wisdom resides, much more than on campus. Church is where students can take their talents and serve. Church has better food, because church has church ladies. In church, students get to celebrate the Lord's Supper and watch babies or adults get baptized.

Church, welcome these kids and find something for them to do when they show up. Get them serving. Feed them. Love them. They are somebody's children, and you could be the answer to a parent's prayer. See if you can find someone to whom you are able to pass that baton.

is the recipient of instructions we still possess in the form of letters. Timothy is a young pastor in a culture that respected age, experience, and wisdom. Can you imagine how encouraging and challenging it was for Timothy to read Paul's personal charge to him, "Don't let anyone look down on you because you are young, but set an example for the believers in speech, in conduct, in love, in faith and in purity" (1 Tim. 4:12)?

The ultimate nonparent adult influence, of course, is Jesus. Jesus shows his disciples what he expects by modeling; he instructs them with fantastic stories; he creates more teachable moments in three years of ministry than we can put together in a lifetime. Jesus knows when to be gentle and is not afraid to be tough. And he pointedly welcomes children when others want to shoo them away.

You might be thinking, "Well, Jesus is God, after all." Yes, he is! But remember his words in the Gospel of John, that he does only the works his Father gave him to do (see John 5:19). Jesus demonstrates reliance on his heavenly Father, as would be right for any other human. He does things that redeemed women and men have the opportunity to do with him, under his grace.

It is still the most astounding fact of history that the apostles (including latecomer Paul) turned the world upside down. If you had told someone that this rabbi from a Roman backwater was going to start a movement with a bunch of fishermen, tax collectors, and a particularly nasty Pharisee and that this movement would outlast the Roman Empire, they would have laughed. I'll bet the laughter sounds just about the same in Greek as it does in English. Chances are the laughter sounds particularly musical in heaven.

Jesus loved those guys, and other disciples to boot. He paid attention to them and never missed an opportunity to pour into their lives. When Jesus was departed from earth, this ragtag group was ready to receive the power of the Holy Spirit and pick up where Jesus left off. They received the baton of faith and became people of influence in the lives of yet another generation. *What will you do with the baton in your hand?*

Don't Default to a Youth Pastor

As mentioned in chapter 3 (about the seven myths), I will always be deeply thankful to the man who ministered long and well to our kids as youth leader. Jonathan Shirk worked as a partner with our family to teach right doctrine, prepare our kids for college, and model what Christian manhood should look like in a husband and father. He was also the consummate goofball, which endeared him not only to our kids but also to Carol and me.

Youth pastors and volunteers with great parachurch ministries, such as Young Life or Youth for Christ, are tremendous allies in raising our kids, but they are inadequate substitutes for us. I fear that we in the church have relinquished much of Christian discipleship to church or parachurch youth programs, which on their best day can't begin to equal what happens at home or in small group fellowships.

Consider the youth worker's job from the perspective of time: youth pastors generally have access to only a fraction of each child's week. Consider the youth worker's job from the perspective of numbers: trying to build meaningful relationships with twenty-five kids! Consider the job from the perspective of influence: a good youth worker or a volunteer may have more of your kid's time for a season, but that season will pass. As a Christian community, we need youth workers, choir directors, Sunday school teachers, and others who serve for seasons in children's lives. Each family within the larger community, however, also needs other adults, ones who relate to our kids throughout the span of their lives.

Remember Your Baptismal (Dedication) Vows

Ted Martin, a local pastor and friend, tells two stories about young men who went AWOL enough from their upbringing and faith so as to get in trouble with the law. Ted was present at the baptism of both and, when things went sour, he remembered the vows taken by the church. The vows sounded something like this: "Do you, the congregation, promise to undertake the responsibility of assisting these parents as they nurture this child in Christian faith and practice to the glory of God?"

Ted never gave up on these fellows, even when one of their fathers, by his own admission, just couldn't be around his son for a season. There was too much pain, too much betrayed trust.

Perhaps you are part of a tradition that does not baptize infants. I assume that you have some means of asking your church if they are on board in helping parents raise kids—a moment in time you can point to, when you said, "Yes!"

Obviously, your children, the ones who abide under your roof, are more your responsibility than anyone else's. This is how God designed the world, ingeniously building a bond between parents and children that will not only perpetuate covenant faith but also carry on the project of developing God's good creation. You may not know much else about what God has called you to do in life, but you can know with certainty that if you have children, you are called to raise them "in the nurture and admonition of the Lord" (Eph. 6:4 KJV).

Since this calling is undeniable and because we live with limited amounts of time, energy, and other resources, we will sometimes have to say no to other things—really good things—to do right by our own children. My mother always had a strong impulse to "fix the world." Yet she lost respect for one of her own heroes, Eleanor Roosevelt, when Mom believed Mrs. Roosevelt had neglected her own family to "save the world."

The call of the Christian to love others, though, extends beyond his or her immediate family. Just as you need the involvement of others in the life of your kids, so others need you to step up for theirs. Start acting as if you believe you are influential in the life of a young person. Although the data suggests this proposition is true, you may have to act your way into believing this truth. After church this week, find a young man or woman in your vicinity,

SARAH WALKO DEPHILLIPS'S STORY

You've read about how the friendship between two families, the Walkos and the Throckmortons, helped create a nurturing environment for their kids. Here is the story of the Walkos's daughter Sarah (now Sarah DePhillips):

I grew up on the outskirts of a small town in southwestern Pennsylvania in a home that was a safe place for me to learn, explore, fall down, and get back up. Both of my grandmothers lived nearby, in fact, and I grew up thinking of my church family as an extension of my immediate family. It seemed like most days of the week I spent time with my church friends, their parents, and/or my grandmother and her friends from church. They certainly treated me like family. I also attended a school pull-out program run by CBM ministries, which is where I accepted Christ.

When I was fifteen (my freshman year of high school), my parents sent me to India—basically by myself. I wasn't too keen on the idea, to tell the truth. But my mother's experience as a Rotary Youth Exchange officer and her contacts in India, as well as her motherly instincts, told her that putting her fifteen-year-old daughter on a plane to a third world country for five weeks in the middle of the school year was a great idea. And she was right. It was five weeks filled with firsts—my first time meeting someone who spoke seven languages, first time eating with my hands and not being chastised, first time seeing an elephant outside a zoo. It was also my first time seeing poverty—real, true poverty. And my first time being away from my family and my church . . . really, truly being on my own in my faith. I grew a lot in that five weeks, living with a host family who had servants and believed in the good luck from burning incense to Krishna, Buddha, Mary, and Jesus figures set up at their family altar.

Postscript: By high school graduation, Sarah had not only been to India but learned more about poverty and justice at a Nazarene youth conference, led a 30 Hour Famine event for her youth group, and heard Gary Haugen, founder and president of the International Justice Mission, speak at the Jubilee Conference. She graduated from Lee University in Cleveland, Tennessee, with a degree in Intercultural Studies (Missiology). Sarah is pursuing a master's degree at Hawaii Pacific University in Global Leadership and Sustainable Development while her husband is stationed on Oahu. She serves with Hoʻōla Nā Pua, a nonprofit that serves underage female sex trafficking victims and raises awareness, and looks forward to being used wherever there is a "need for the light of God's Kingdom and the Hope of his Redemption."

shake hands, and initiate a conversation. Learn the young person's name; show an interest. Pray for this person throughout the week, and look for the opportunity to greet him or her next week.

When you are with another family, spend some time catching up with a member of the next generation. Ask questions. Listen. Expect God to show up. Consider showing up yourself at the kid's track meet or theater production.

Surprised by Research: Again

Do you know who gets this whole "influence of adults" thing in spades? The Latter-day Saints (LDS), also known as the Mormons. As a result, Mormon kids are statistically more likely than kids raised as Christians to "stick" with their faith into adulthood.

Curious to understand this reality, Kenda Creasy Dean, who was involved in the original NSYR team, studied the practices of the LDS church and reported on them in her book *Almost Christian*.[2] Dean's interest is not only in creating structures that help kids and the church adhere to one another but also in more faithfully passing along the *content* of our Christian faith.

What do the LDS folks do that Christian parents can learn from? Some practices are not surprising because the reputation of Mormon families is to be very close. Families pray together and connect purposefully with the broader LDS community. Monday nights are officially family nights—it is not permissible to schedule other church activities, as parents are supposed to be home with their kids.

At about age fifteen, Mormon kids are asked to take it up a notch. In just a few years they will have the opportunity to go on a two-year mission, particularly encouraged for LDS men. It is time to get ready. So for four years, they attend early morning "seminary," five days a week.

Seminary combines practices, such as journaling deeply into one's faith, with practical exercises for preparing for the two-year mission of service and evangelism. And according to Dean, it is often taught by a . . . parent! Someone took the idea of what "high commitment parenting" looks like and raised the ante.

Here is how Dean describes the outcome:

> All of these experiences—demanding programs of religious educa-
> tion, peer accountability for living according to Mormon norms,
> family activities that emphasize Mormon distinctiveness, participa-
> tion in Mormon missions—impress on Latter-Day Saints young
> people that Mormonism is not an activity they choose nor a church
> they attend. It is literally a way of life and affects every choice they
> make.[3]

For many Christian kids, their faith is not a way of life but an extracurricular activity or like a hobby. This is the model they observe in their families. My point here is not necessarily that we need to raise the bar for our kids (though we do) but that we need to expect more from ourselves. We need to be intentionally influential in the lives of kids in our church community. We need to invite adults from that community to be influential in the lives of our kids.

As parents, we also can communicate that we expect our kids to step up and embrace their faith, even in college. As your kids transition to college, make attending church one of the "essentials" you request of your kids. Whether to go will ultimately be their decision, but let them know you will be asking, "So how was church this week?" Hopefully, they will choose to go to church, encounter caring adults of various ages, and also find opportunities to serve.

The Boo Radley Principle

Spoiler alert! If you have read *To Kill a Mockingbird* or seen the movie—both equally good—this illustration will mean something to you, but if you haven't, skip this part. You need to read the book or see the movie and will be deprived until you do. I'm about to reveal the plot, so if Atticus Finch is not yet a favorite of yours, catch me again in the next chapter.

If it has been a while since you read or saw *To Kill a Mockingbird*, which takes place in the 1930s, here is the basic plot:

Atticus Finch, played by Gregory Peck in the film, is an attorney and widower with two children. Jem is ten years old when the story begins and thirteen when it ends. His sister, Jean Louise aka Scout, is four years younger than Jem. Scout is the narrator as well as a key character in this story by author Harper Lee.

Scout and Jem have many adventures and misadventures with another youngster nicknamed Dill, who spends summers in their small Alabama town. All three kids have a nearly obsessive focus on the Finches' neighbor, Boo Radley, played by Robert Duvall in his first big movie role.

From a child's perspective, Boo is a creepy neighbor. He is a grown man who lives with his parents and has not been seen outside for many years. Only his family knows exactly what Boo looks like now, or what exactly is wrong with him.

Jem and Scout begin to find small treasures like sticks of gum in the knot of a tree in front of the Radley place. The kids suspect Boo might be putting them there at night just for them, but if so, what are his motives? Though they are afraid of him, the kids sneak around the house, hoping to get a glimpse of Boo through the window or trying to lure him outside.

One late October night, Scout and Jem are heading home in the dark from a Halloween event, cutting through the rocky field between the local school and their house. Jem thinks he hears someone following them, and before they are quite home, Scout is attacked. Her brother tries to rescue her, but the attacker, a grown man, tosses Jem aside and Jem's arm breaks. A mysterious someone rescues them both before something really awful happens—a big, strong someone.

That's right. It's the über-creepy Boo Radley. It turns out Boo is simple, but he is good.

I think it's high time Boo had something named after him, so I declare the Boo Radley Principle: *Any adult can figure out how to help a child if that adult will simply pay attention.* Boo was paying attention and he knew how to help. "Of course he paid attention," you say, "because that was all Boo had to do." That's the point. What are we doing these days that has us so busy and moving so fast that we are missing the needs of the people around us, particularly the kids? Have we become like those religious types in the parable of the Good Samaritan, who see the obvious need of a neighbor but just scoot right by?

You have the power to be a person of positive influence in the life of a young person. Use your power for good!

8

Invite Kids

Guide Your Kids from Peer Pressure to Peer Positive

Wanted: Friend for twelve-year-old child. Must have a clean criminal record and, if at all possible, have discovered personal hygiene. "Please" and "Thank you" a must, but Eddie Haskell types (of Leave It to Beaver *fame) need not apply. Desirable but not necessary that he or she be a Christian. Gaming or social media threshold for acceptable candidates less than two hours a day. We will provide snacks, oversight, and a safe environment. Applicants may be asked for a urine sample. Please respond to marcy@overthetopmom.net.*

If only we could pick our kids' friends, wouldn't life be easier? Humans, after all, become like those with whom they spend time. No wonder the writer of Proverbs so emphasizes the importance of choosing good companions: "Whoever walks with the wise becomes wise, but the companion of fools will suffer harm" (Prov. 13:20 ESV). The importance of the choices we and our kids make about friends and influential acquaintances cannot be overstated. Our very characters are at stake.

Although it may seem strange in our individualistic culture, Scripture *endorses* peer relationships as part of God's design. When functioning as they should, peer relationships support us, hold us accountable, and encourage us toward healthy character and good works. What's more, friendships and other forms of human community can have redemptive power in our lives. They provide us, and our children with us, the opportunity to share Jesus with the world through our love for one another.

Of course, peer relationships are often shallow, or places where we get hurt. This can lead us to isolate, robbing our children and ourselves of the positive influences we discussed in the last chapter. Thus, we need to be intentional about our peer relationships and present a healthy model to our children.

I suggest we think of childhood and adolescence as the learning ground for friendships. As they grow, our kids' own choices serve as a sort of practice field, where they build the insight and skills needed to make wise relational decisions in college and beyond. The relationships they choose in and after college will have a huge impact on the people our children become.

The Case for Relationships

Imagine God making something from nothing and then forming that something into stars, galaxies, and this amazing planet. In Genesis 1 and 2, we see a refrain of delight coming from the Lord himself after each day of creation—six times God says, "It is good."

As God sees Adam at work in the garden, however, God spots something out of sync, not as it should be. He proclaims, "It is not good for the man to be alone" (Gen. 2:18). God makes a helper, a companion, from the man, so that male and female are of the same essence.

This is the first place in the Scripture where we see human community. "It is not good for the man to be alone" certainly applies to marriage, but Eve is also the first "other," the being who makes human relationships possible. Whether married or single, child or adult, it is neither normative nor healthy for human beings to be isolated. As the seventeenth-century English poet John Donne wrote, "No man is an island."

In the twenty-first century, we have the benefit of research showing what happens to people who don't have enough social contact. They become depressed and experience higher rates of obesity and lower brain function. It's not good. In fact, writing this book has put me into necessary periods of isolation, and it is now a race to see what happens first—finishing or developing an invisible friend!

The impulse to create human community comes from a God who exists forever in divine community. To plumb the depths of the Trinity—Father, Son, and Holy Spirit—is beyond my skill, but it is apparent, particularly from the Gospels, that Jesus and the Father have loved one another from eternity. God the Holy Spirit delights to do the will of both the Father and the Son. This is a unified trio, as evidenced by Jesus's prayer in John 17:21, that the church would be one, even as he and the Father are one.

Humans are made to be in community with God and each other. You, and your children with you, are actually designed by God in a way that not only allows the influence of others but actually invites it.

We may bristle at the idea of needing community and prefer to go it alone. Relationships are complicated and, as I mentioned earlier, usually the place where we are most deeply wounded. Most kids find peer relationships hard, and adults have their own set of issues with other people: the coworker who doesn't pull his weight, the neighbor who makes excessive noise late at night, the friend who deserts us, the parent who never says (or said), "I love you," or the spouse who treats us with contempt.

Psalm 55, like many biblical prayers, is a cry to God from a desperate human. The poem reaches a painful and startling climax halfway in when the composer stops addressing God and talks directly to the person who has wounded him.

> If it were an enemy making fun of me,
> I could endure it;
> if it were an opponent boasting over me,
> I could hide myself from him.
> But it is you, my companion,
> my colleague and close friend.
> We had intimate talks with each other
> and worshiped together in the Temple. (Ps. 55:12–14 GNT)

If you or your child shy away from peer friendships, remember that no one has experienced relational brokenness more deeply than Jesus. Our Lord welcomed many disciples, but the twelve explicitly mentioned in Scripture were especially close to him (see Matt. 10:1–4). Among them was Judas. Churchgoers have heard the account of the Last Supper and the Garden of Gethsemane so often that we are numb to the hurt Judas causes Jesus when he betrays him, selling Jesus out for thirty pieces of silver (see Luke 22:1–6, 47–48).

Further, the moment of separation Jesus endures on the cross—"My God, my God, why have you forsaken me?" (Matt. 27:46)—gives Jesus a perspective on intimacy and loss that will always be deeper than the worst we can experience.

Even though Jesus knew betrayal and separation were coming, throughout his ministry he modeled and described a relational life full of hope and power. Jesus rooted all his teaching in the second part of the great commandment, "Love your neighbor as yourself" (Matt. 22:39). When challenged by a law expert on exactly who is worthy to be considered our neighbor, Jesus told the parable of the Good Samaritan (see Luke 10:25–37). This parable turns the tables by replacing "Who is my neighbor?" with "To whom can I be a neighbor?" Although the parable cannot be reduced to a simple modern saying, it does bring this one to mind: to have a real friend, *be* a real friend.

Whether we isolate ourselves because we have had bad experiences in relationships, are very shy, or just don't feel the need for other people, we do so swimming against the tide of Scripture and

IT TAKES A VILLAGE TO RAISE . . . ME

I have raised the white flag—I cannot do this Christ-as-Lord thing alone. I need support, and an almost embarrassing amount of it, to follow Jesus daily. I talk to two guys every Thursday morning from 6:30 to 7:30. I have breakfast with two other guys on Fridays. I meet or speak regularly with older and wiser men. I have lunch once or twice a month with two peers. I spend as much time with my wife as our schedules allow; we go on dates with our calendars to plan more dates we can put on our calendars. Hey, quality time is a love language for both of us, and we can only get it by planning. Carol and I recently joined a couple's small group because we want to grow more together.

Professionally, I'm part of a group of CEOs who meet monthly to sharpen our leadership skills, and I have dinner once a month with another group of leaders who are Christians.

Mine is the relational map for an extroverted person, to be sure. If I were not so socially wired, the number of people with whom I meet—the web of relationship—would be smaller. That would be okay, as long as I was invested in a relational web of some size.

Take an inventory of your relational life and consider what it tells you. If it looks a little lean, make it a priority to have lunch with a friend periodically or to have someone over after church. Ask someone to get together and pray. If you are a man, you will almost certainly need to take things up a notch—most of us men are too isolated. You not only will rediscover forgotten joys (and challenges!) but will encourage your child to experience what it really means to be part of the body of Christ.

If you are a woman, allow yourself the luxury of at least one close friendship outside of your home. If you are a single parent and feeling the pressure to allocate every minute of your day effectively, make building a good relationship with at least one of your peers a priority. This is not being selfish but rather modeling something very sweet for your kids.

our very nature. Our enjoyment of friendships and other forms of human community is one of the best gifts we can give our own children, and one of the most important. How might you best model this for your kids?

The Positive Power of Peer Influence

The best antidote for the negative peer influence many parents fear is itself peer influence. Friends who shape our kids can also be friends who protect them, even as our children do the same for their friends. The writer of Ecclesiastes says, "Though one may be overpowered, two can defend themselves. A cord of three strands is not quickly broken" (4:12).

Notice that the writer of Ecclesiastes does not encourage rugged individualism here but rather points out how much stronger a group is than a single person. There may be a time when our child is on his or her own and must stand up when no one else will, but this is the exception. Our primary message to our kids should not be, "It is you against the world." No, the primary message should be, "Find like-minded friends with whom you can not only stand for what is right but influence the beliefs, attitudes, and behaviors of others."

College students who have learned how to choose positive peer influences before they arrive on campus have a distinct advantage. They are more likely to look for Christian fellowship, build good relationships, and navigate the difficulties of higher education successfully. Whether it is the temptation to party excessively or challenges to Christian faith from a professor, Christian students who are connected with other Christian students are much more likely—exponentially more likely—to not only survive but grow as a follower of Christ.

Every so often I get put on the spot with a question like, "What's the most important factor in my son or daughter making it through college as a Christian?" My visceral response from years of this work is the need to be connected to other Christians. Before I can stop myself, it comes out: "The isolated become roadkill."

The opposite is also true. Alyssa is now a missionary in a predominately Muslim country in the Mediterranean. As an undergraduate, she led the largest and most recognized student organization on her thirty-five-thousand-student campus. From her first year on, Alyssa was part of a thriving Christian fellowship, where she built friendships with men and women who continue to support and encourage her from thousands of miles away. She says, "I was a leader as an undergraduate and have taken the risk to work overseas as a direct result of the people that God has put in my life. It's true of my campus ministers, but just as true for my peers—I would never have become who I am now apart from them."

Childhood: Training Ground for Healthy Relationships

Throughout elementary school and adolescence, friends will have an impact on our kids' character, but parents will remain primary influencers. College students, on the other hand, experience disproportionately large peer influences. Nearly all of their daily contact comes from men and women who are, roughly speaking, the same age. There is no family in the dorm, and most kids will not become close enough with a faculty member to have anything like a parent around. As I mentioned in the last chapter, some congregations embrace college students into the life of the church, but they are not the norm.

Yes, most students room with and go to class, play, study, and party with peers. By the time your son or daughter gets to college, the need to choose friends well is a huge priority. How does it begin?

In the previous chapter, we considered how the relationship between your family and other families can help introduce your kids to influential, caring adults. Many of those adults have kids of their own. The children of people you like and respect are good candidates for friendship with your own kids.

When Harvard professor Robert Putnam did follow-up research to his groundbreaking book *Bowling Alone*, he discovered that "in 1975 the average American entertained friends at home 15 times per year; the equivalent figure (1998) is now barely half that."[1] Perhaps we feel more isolated as families because we *are* more isolated. To get un-isolated, clean the grill, buy the watermelon, and invite another family or two over.

As your children express interest in kids you (or they) don't know, invite these children to your house. Get to know them and, if possible, get to know their parents. As you have probably learned from experience, most of the kids you meet are a lot like your own sons or daughters: they have lots of energy, vivid imaginations, and love to play. They are also open to the influence of other caring adults, which might just describe you!

As your kids meet peers outside the circle of those you know, introduce them to Scripture's wisdom on the matter of choosing friends. The book of Proverbs paints vivid pictures of bad peer influences and has encouraging words relative to wise friends. It's hard to read Proverbs without concluding that the age of Solomon's intended audience for the book is early adolescence. This may be why the appeals to young men in particular carry urgency. Consider Solomon's words to a youngster who has made an unwise pledge to a neighbor:

> So do this, my son, to free yourself,
>   since you have fallen into your neighbor's hands:
> Go—to the point of exhaustion—
>   and give your neighbor no rest!
> Allow no sleep to your eyes,
>   no slumber to your eyelids.
> Free yourself, like a gazelle from the hand of the hunter,
>   like a bird from the snare of the fowler. (Prov. 6:3–5)

Through Scripture, the friendships you model, and conversation, help your child to build the insights and skills to choose positive peer relationships in college and beyond.

Here are a few ideas parents have found helpful in surrounding their kids with other children likely to be good influences:

- Make your house the place kids want to come, and do everything you can to make them feel welcome. Hint: a few games to play and *good* snacks.
- Help coach a team, become part of a parent-teacher organization, or become part of Boy or Girl Scouts, Indian Guides, and so on.
- Encourage involvement in a parachurch organization such as Young Life or Youth for Christ.
- Expose your child to a good Christian summer camp.

What Can We Learn from the Church in Zimbabwe?

J. B. Sibanda had a few things to adjust to when he and his son Milton moved to the United States. J. B. had been a youth pastor at his church in Zimbabwe, so it took a while to learn that by "youth" the church in America means essentially "high school-aged." The Zimbabwean church, like much of Africa, is a youthful church—most members are under age forty. When they talk about the "youth group" in Zimbabwe, or at least at J. B.'s church, they mean people between the *ages of twelve and thirty-five.*

So what are the outcomes of having a youth ministry that spans twenty-three years? Well, for one thing, young people in Zimbabwe are involved in nearly every aspect of the church. In the States, we seem to end up with invisible populations—those we don't seem to know what to do with, like college students home on break or post-college singles. The probability of this dilemma is much lower in J. B.'s home church.

Another positive in the broad-ranging youth ministry is the opportunity for kids at one level of maturity to invest in the lives of those less mature. In the United States, this would often mean college-aged or post-college young adults investing in high school students, who in turn "mentor" middle school students, who may actually serve elementary school kids. Interestingly, it is a model that parachurch ministries like Young Life and the CCO have used for years, to great effect. It is also what gives summer camps their structure. Younger campers look up to and emulate older campers. If a kid attends camp for enough years, he or she can eventually be some kind of assistant, then a camp counselor.

Conducting my parent focus groups, I encountered two churches where this kind of discipling culture was in evidence, and it was powerful. From middle school on, there is an emphasis on not only having mentors, teachers, and role models but also being just such a person for the next group down. That means middle schoolers spending time with elementary-aged kids, high schoolers investing in middle schoolers, college students mentoring high school students, and post-college adults lifting up college students. *The churches have not so much created a program but an environment and a set of practices that allow this discipleship to happen fairly naturally.*

One of my mentors, Sibyl Towner, calls this *leveled, layered leadership* (LLL). Here, I believe, are the underlying reasons why LLL is so powerful:

1. Even from a young age, kids learn to serve others.
2. LLL creates a pathway for discipleship. A Christian who knows more than the child takes the child under his or her wing to learn. That child does the same for those behind him or her.
3. LLL gives a youth group staying power, and makes it less dependent on the charisma of the youth pastor.

As parents, we may not be able to reorganize our church's Christian education program and youth ministry, but we can make some moves in this direction on our own. We can take advantage of what is present in our own home if we have more than one child. Catch your kids in the act of being a good example to younger siblings or showing a younger brother or sister kindness. Stoke the fire of influence with your kids—*their* influence. Reinforce the message by talking about the effect they have when they extend themselves on behalf of other people.

It might sound like this:

> Jane, I saw you take Zoe in the house for ice cream when the Winsproggles were over the other day. You treated her with kindness and helped make her whole day better. I think Zoe was probably nervous when she got here, but your consideration changed all that. You have also given her a great example of how to treat kids younger than you. Someday Zoe will probably do the same for someone else. Isn't that cool?!

Broken down:

1. Catch your child doing something good.
2. Name and affirm what the child has done.
3. Tell them about the impact.

This is not just how kids gain confidence to serve others; it is how all of us gain confidence. The best leaders use this model to help those in their charge grow in character and capacity. Look closely at any high-functioning organization and you will find someone naming and affirming the actions of others.

Also look for contexts where your child can be both the one served and the one serving. In bigger youth ministries, this can often happen in small groups, which parents can convene and even lead. The small group allows for deeper relationships and for the emergence of good peer influence.

This kind of connection, one Christian knowing and loving another, is how we show our love to the world. See once again the words of Jesus: "By this everyone will know that you are my disciples, if you love one another" (John 13:35).

Persistent Bad Peer Choices Require Parental Intervention

A time may come when you need to have a hard conversation with your son or daughter about a kid you don't believe is a good influence. Setting and keeping safe boundaries is the un-fun but necessary part of parenting. If your son or daughter has a friendship that seems toxic, it may be necessary to use parental authority and essentially say, "No, you cannot go there." The conversation with a preteen might sound something like this.

> **Mom:** "It seems like whenever you come home from Joey's house you talk back to me, don't do what I ask, and are mean to your sister. We have talked about Joey before and about the kinds of friends that can make us better people as opposed to worse ones. Which kind of friend do you think Joey is?"
>
> **Son:** "I don't think I do any of those things. I like hanging out with Joey."
>
> **Mom:** "I understand, but since we have talked about this before and nothing has changed, I want you to take a break from going to Joey's."
>
> **Son:** "You mean I can't go over there at all? Can he come over here?"
>
> **Mom:** "Right now, neither. I don't think I will ever be comfortable allowing you to go to Joey's house. In a month we can discuss having Joey over here. Let's write it on the calendar so we don't forget."
>
> **Son:** "Oh, man, this is so unfair!"
>
> **Mom:** "I'm sorry, son, but all of us tend to become like the people we spend time with. I'm not saying Joey is a rotten kid, but I don't like what happens when you are around him a lot. Can you think of someone else you would like to ask over?"

You may find your son or daughter is relieved to have permission to lessen or break off regular contact with certain of his or her peers. Help your child do it graciously.

Of course, this conversation is easier with younger kids, but what if you don't like who your teenager is hanging around? This is more serious, and it may become necessary to consider actions that are more drastic. As much as your kids may chafe when you do it, talk to them about it. Name the problem as you see it. Affirm and love your child but don't let the situation go on. A bad crowd in middle or high school can take your son or daughter to dangerous places.

The core message of this book is that, contrary to popular myth, parents are more influential than anyone or anything else when it comes to preparing their children for college. But most developmental experts note that peer influence *does* grow during the teenage years. In fact, we may find that our warnings about certain kids we perceive to be bad influences have the opposite effect from what we have intended. Our children may rebel and be even more determined to seek out those about whom Scripture would say, "Bad company corrupts good character" (1 Cor. 15:33). If your child is now in harm's way—experimenting with (or addicted to) drugs or alcohol or becoming sexually active, for example—it might be necessary to think of previously unthinkable options.

Switching schools is a big move, particularly if your child doesn't want to do it. But if he or she really is in with the wrong crowd, consider this an option. It is important to be honest with yourself, your spouse, and your child. What is likely to happen if something doesn't change? Change often feels riskier to us than the status quo because we have not taken into account what the status quo will likely bring our way. What might happen if your child is on a bad trajectory that goes uninterrupted?

Change can come in many forms, and it will work best if you work through it with your teenager. But if they are putting themselves or others in danger, you might have to investigate options your son or daughter won't like. When it comes to schooling alternatives, don't assume a Catholic or other Christian school is out of reach financially. Look at some options, narrow things down, and talk with an admissions person about financial aid.

I have two vivid memories from sixth and seventh grade, when I was often in trouble. One was taking the entry test for a private school, which for me as a city public school kid was humiliating. The second was finding a brochure for Culver Military Academy in our mailbox one day, sent to our home by request of my parents. Man, this was getting serious! These events, combined with other "tough love" responses from Mom and Dad (such as being grounded until I was thirty—I had it coming!), eventually helped me "straighten up and fly right."

Another option is to stay in the same school, but not with the same people. If your child will at least agree that they are in with

JESUS RESTORING FRIENDSHIP

When Jesus walked the earth, he had friends.

He also demonstrated the efforts we should make to restore a broken friendship. Each time I read the postresurrection accounts in the Gospels, I wonder how a human could be more defeated than Peter was after he denied knowing Jesus three times. Peter had been confident that he would stick close to Jesus, but when it counted most, Peter buckled. "Then Peter remembered the word the Lord had spoken to him: 'Before the rooster crows today, you will disown me three times.' And he went outside and wept bitterly" (Luke 22:61–62). Then Jesus died and there seemed no hope for Peter to be reconciled with his master and friend.

It would be hopeless if there were no resurrection. Yet, who among the remaining eleven disciples did Jesus choose to be the first to witness the empty tomb? Peter. (See Luke 24:12; 1 Cor. 15:5.) A little while later, Peter was fishing when a mysterious stranger showed up on shore and recommended trying a different spot. The resulting harvest of 153 big fish reminded one of Peter's friends (most certainly John) of another miracle catch, which happened right before Jesus invited Peter to fish for men instead of fish (see Luke 5:1–11). This time Peter, in typical Peter fashion, jumped out of the boat a hundred yards from shore and waded in.

The scene that follows is as poignant as one in any book or movie, and it also goes a long way to explaining why Peter is still around on the day of Pentecost when the Holy Spirit comes. Jesus is on the shore, cooking breakfast for his friends, when Peter wades in. As they share a meal in front of the fire (see John 21:15–17), Jesus asks Peter three times, "Simon a bad crowd, they may be willing to try a new extracurricular activity—a club (debate, chess), a sport, band, drama—where the kids involved are either of better character or just too busy to get in trouble. Once summer break comes, stoke the good influences and starve the bad ones. If it means sacrificing some summer job income to make room for Young Life camp, a wilderness experience in the mountains, or a long family vacation, do it.

With all I've written here about great peer influences, I may seem rather callous to the needs of young people who are far from

son of John, do you love me?" Notice that Peter has gone back to his old name, temporarily losing the manly moniker, "Rock."

This is a painful scene for Peter, his discomfort growing with each repeated question. By the third "Do you love me?" he is hurt and exasperated ("How many times is Jesus going to ask me this?"). He answers, "Lord, you know all things; you know that I love you."

This is the last time Jesus asks Peter the question. For every denial there is one "Do you love me?" and one admonition, "Care for [feed] my sheep." After predicting how Peter will die, Jesus restores his relationship with Peter by reissuing that initial invitation, "Follow me!" (John 21:19).

We typically read this passage as Peter's reinstatement to disciple (now apostle) status, and that does seem to be the main point. But this event also serves as the restoration of a very human friendship. Peter has wounded his rabbi and friend at Jesus's deepest point of vulnerability. Only God turning his head away ("My God, my God, why have you forsaken me?") cuts deeper than Peter's denial. These words echo David's words from Psalm 55:13, which we read earlier: "But it is you, my companion, my colleague and close friend."

In this exchange, Jesus not only restores one of his three closest disciples, he creates a powerful example of relational restoration. He creates his own real-life parable about "loving your neighbor as yourself." He lives into his own prayer to forgive those who sin against us (see Matt. 6:12). Jesus shows us that even when it might seem impossible to get a friend back who has betrayed us, there is great hope. He shows us that the power of the resurrection breathes hope into every part of life, even the most broken relationship between friends.

God or whose lives are a mess. But there is a way for your child to touch lost or hurting peers.

Reaching the Lost through Community

When Christians do this "love one another" thing, they model what is both rare and highly desirable. "I don't know exactly what it is, but I want some of that!" Healthy Christian community is our megaphone to reach the world. Show me a place where many are coming to new faith in Christ, and I will show you a group of loving Christians making the kingdom of God real, bringing a part of heaven to earth.

Here's a story that illustrates the principle. Branden Kummer is a journalism major at Point Park University, a growing school of four thousand located in downtown Pittsburgh. Until recently Branden described himself as a hard-line atheist. He stumbled into friendships with Christian students because, on his first day on campus, one of those students invited him to attend a meeting of The Body, the CCO-sponsored fellowship on campus.

Branden says, "I went to three or four meetings and decided I wasn't interested in hearing any more about God." A semester later, he ran into one of the students he'd met at The Body and was invited to return. Branden showed up at a meeting and hasn't stopped going since.

Branden insists that he wouldn't still be at Point Park if it weren't for the community he found at The Body. "They didn't care that I didn't believe," he says. "When it comes to my beliefs, or my lack of them, I'm not quiet about it. They're really great people. I never intended to open myself up to what they had to say, but it kind of happened."

Branden attended the CCO's annual Jubilee Conference one February, treating it as a journalism assignment. When the conference ended, however, Branden was a different person. At Jubilee, he had committed his life to Jesus Christ.

What attracted Branden in the first place? The Body was a loving, cohesive community that could model the Christian life—a group with a solid core. Branden needed to hear the gospel, but he also needed to see it lived out in loving community.

This is the invitation your child can give to his or her friends who don't know Jesus—"Come and be with us."

Where Peers Can Take Us

It was an early fall weekend morning in New England, many miles and many years from John and Laurie's wedding in 1985. Dave had been a groomsman when John and Laurie were married, and he was in their home with his family for a visit, as were Carol and I.

Dave started reading a letter John had written to all of his groomsmen—a letter that hadn't surfaced in thirty years. I know John, Dave, most of the other groomsmen, and their wives. They have kept their friendships—and their marriages—through the years of rearing children, working multiple jobs, making moves, and experiencing both heartaches and victories. They present a beautiful picture of enduring friendship. Here is the letter:

June 14, 1985

Gentlemen,

As the most important day of my Christian life draws near, I find myself, more than ever, reflecting on the grace of the God which has been so richly evident in my life. Certainly not the least of His blessings has been your friendship. I cannot begin to imagine what life would have been like without your collective impact on me. Besides Jesus Himself I have valued nothing more than our relationships, one with another. Nothing has challenged, supported, encouraged, and strengthened my faith in Christ more than you. Nothing has brought more joy, fulfillment, and sheer delight to me than the many experiences we have shared. To a large degree I am who I am today because of the Lord working through you. . . . If a man were to be judged solely on the quality of character in his friends, I would be foremost among men. As David said to Jonathan, so too, I can say of you, "More precious has your love been than that of any woman." I love you guys!"

9

Christian Kids Can Thrive through College

Parents frequently share with me their fears surrounding college and their kids. Parents ask, "Is it possible for a young man or woman who is a Christian to survive college, faith intact?"

My answer is, "Yes!" Still, I'm not sure it is the right question.

Every month a report comes across my desk with stories of students, some of whom came to college with a faith and many of whom did not. These stories usually have plenty of ups and downs, and they often track with someone who has been through a crisis. What they have in common is their honest portrayal of young people who are not just surviving college as Christians, but thriving.

When I use the word *thriving*, the quick definition that comes to mind is "healthy with the capacity for growth." The definition we considered in chapter 2 is a picture of a woman or man who is thriving: *The young adult Christian owns his or her faith in Jesus Christ, reflects it in priorities and decisions, and lives it in community with other believers, seeking to influence the watching world.*

I'm not suggesting that college is without its share of difficulties. Parents are concerned about the hostility of American higher education to religious faith for good reasons. While I was writing this book, the entire California State University system stopped recognizing Christian fellowships on campus whose only fault was to insist that their leaders actually be Christians. (Two years later, the order was rescinded and ministries such as InterVarsity were welcomed back.)

Alcohol is still the great social lubricant on most of our campuses and is now accompanied by binge drinking. The relationship between alcohol consumption, casual sex, and sexual violence against women is well documented, but no one seems to know what to do about it.

External threats like this are one thing, but of course there is the question of each child's readiness to handle the incredible freedom that comes with college. I have two in school this semester and right now, on Friday night, they could be doing anything—unless they post it on Facebook or choose to share it with Carol and me, we will never know.

Yes, I've seen the obstacles and the tripwires.

What makes me so confident students can thrive in college, particularly in light of the kinds of challenges young people face these days? First, I rely on the nature of God and the truth of Scripture. God loves and pursues college students, and Scripture affirms repeatedly that God's affections toward his children are unchanging. I hold fast to Scriptures, such as Philippians 1:6, where Paul encourages the church: "He who began a good work in you will carry it on to completion until the day of Christ Jesus." This reminds me that God is not done with our children as they transition to college. Neither is he done with parents as they transition to empty nests.

Then there are the real-life college student accounts I referred to at the beginning of the chapter: example upon example of men and women of varying backgrounds who develop into whole human beings and devoted Christ-followers during college. Along with current students, I have the accounts of those who made a major move toward God several decades ago and are continuing to grow in loving God and loving their neighbor.

Here is the report from just a few relatively recent graduates, two women and two men—a graduate student, a teacher, an actuary, and a soldier, each of whom grew in big ways during college. I've not chosen these examples all that carefully—they were first in the stack of hundreds. Meet Ris, Gabi, Jeff, and Jacob.

As an indecisive and impatient person, my faith has allowed me to be more confident and patient with my decisions. It has been five years since I accepted Jesus into my life, and I did not picture myself being where I am now. Through prayer, the decisions that I've made were not my will, but they were God's will, and because He reveals His goodness and faithfulness every day, I know I can trust Him more.

Ris Nakajima, Allegheny College, 2011

From every soccer game I played in, to interviews, to now working as a student teacher, I give glory to God and I do my best to apply His values to what I'm doing. Right now, I am student teaching seventh grade science in an inner-city public school, and it is a roller coaster! Some days I am so high and other days I want to cry. But I know that at the end of either day, I have to bring it back to God. I have to remember that He is in control.

Gabi Ingram, Kent State, 2012

Coming back to the church during college grew my faith and relationship with Christ. The ministry of the CCO helped me to understand that knowing about God doesn't mean I truly know Him. It's a relationship, and I need to take what I know and apply it to my prayer life, my personal life, and my work life.

Jeff Winkler, Penn State, 2007

My faith was the bedrock that kept me strong through four years in the Army, including a deployment to Afghanistan. CCO ministries always encouraged me in my calling to be a part of the military after college and gave me strength in difficult and trying times overseas in a war zone. My faith allowed me to better reconcile with the Afghans that I met and dealt with and was instrumental in any and all successes I had over there.

Jacob Portnoff, Carnegie Mellon University, U.S. Army

Kids clearly can mature and blossom spiritually in college, but it's not an automatic outcome. Once again, how parents claim and practice their influence before and during college will make a big difference. Although the child's choices determine the ultimate outcome, parents definitely have influence.

Before we dig into practical actions you can take as a parent to prepare your child for the special challenges of college, let's look at why college actually is prime time for kids to grasp their faith and grow in positive new ways.

College Is a Great Place for Christian Discipleship

I've had only rare conversations with high school students about the material they are encountering in the classroom, the meaning of what they are learning, and how they feel about it. Take those same men and women following their first year of college, and the level of engagement with ideas is completely different.

Perhaps the need to take responsibility for oneself as a collegian explains the change. Perhaps it is the natural process of brain development and emotional maturing. I'm not exactly sure, but the pattern is unmistakable—college is when most young people start to figure things out and, as a consequence, can move from a passive consumer to a responsible grown-up when it comes to learning.

This active disposition toward learning will certainly help when it comes to getting and keeping a job, raising kids, and so on. But it is bigger than that. The call to follow Jesus is also a call to

"Take my yoke upon you and learn from me" (Matt. 11:29). When Paul admonishes ("See to it that no one takes you captive through hollow and deceptive philosophy" [Col. 2:8]) or encourages ("Be transformed by the renewing of your mind" [Rom. 12:2]), he is assuming his audience will be accountable to learn his teaching and put it into practice. Paul's instructions to the Philippian church follow this pattern: "Keep putting into practice all you learned and received from me—everything you heard from me and saw me doing" (Phil. 4:9 NLT).

College students have an increased capacity for learning, growing, accountability, and a fresh humility that makes them teachable. This humility also leads them to the front door of thankfulness. We've devoted a good chunk of space to this topic throughout the book. A young teen often lacks awareness, particularly as it relates to expressing gratitude. In my experience, the penny finally drops during college. It could be the longing for a home-cooked meal, a comfy bed, and a bit more privacy that gets the gratitude train moving. For our boys, it was the realization that not everyone had the opportunity to grow up in a home where "I love you" was a regular part of everyday life. Jack and Spence both got to live adjacent to others who had different experiences from theirs. This deepened their appreciation for Carol, me, and the environment we provided in our home.

Learning to feel and express gratitude is bedrock to the Christian faith. We are those who have been "bought at a price" (1 Cor. 6:20). We are charged with giving "thanks in all circumstances" (1 Thess. 5:18). Whatever causes the phenomenon, college students are usually growing significantly in gratitude.

College is also the place where the world gets bigger. Some of this comes from the classroom, where the number and variety of offerings, to say nothing of the men and women who teach, provides a college student with the chance to explore the wider world. It could be a class on ballroom dancing, African history, the Catalan language, or physical geology.

Interaction with other students also expands your child's horizons, usually in positive ways. Their roommates and classmates are often from other states (or countries), possibly with a different regional culture, and certainly with a different family culture. Each time your son or daughter rubs up against these differences, his or her world expands.

With exposure to other people and cultures, our children learn to be more empathetic and less judgmental. A bigger view of the world will also often be accompanied by a bigger perception of God, a deeper understanding of God's mercy, and eyes newly opened to the lordship of Jesus Christ over everything.

Now let's look at those practical actions you can take as a parent to prepare your child for the special challenges of college.

The Challenge of Dualism:
Prepare by Helping Your Child to Recognize It

The expanding world is good news for your Christian child, unless he or she gets trapped into dualistic thinking. For many parents, exposure to dualism is a hidden danger in the lives of their college kids. This danger is as real as any of the others that strike fear into the hearts of Christian parents, and you need to prepare your child to think clearly about the difference between dualism and Christianity.

Dualism is a worldview that divides the world into two distinct parts, typically labeled "sacred and secular" or "spiritual and profane." In this worldview, God cares about the sacred—consisting of worship, studying Scripture, praying, sharing our faith, and so on. God doesn't care so much about the other part—consisting of work (unless we are pastors, missionaries, and so on), eating, sleeping, playing, and reproducing.

Dualistic thinking contrasts sharply with the message of Scripture that says, "The earth is the LORD's and the fullness thereof, the world and those who dwell therein" (Ps. 24:1 ESV) and "God was pleased to have all this fullness dwell in [Christ], and through him to reconcile to himself all things, whether things on earth or things in heaven" (Col. 1:20). We have marching orders, based on God's ownership of everything, to work at whatever we do with all our hearts (see Col. 3:23).

Scripture doesn't recognize sacred and secular: it is all one, and all alike belongs to God. In fact, God owns everything twice—once by virtue of creating it and second by purchasing it back from the vagaries of sin.

Because dualism is a perspective rather than a religion, your college student may not recognize it as a danger. It may slip in as an assumed fact in course material or in the behavior of other students. As a parent of a college-bound child, it's important for you to learn and talk about dualism with your child. Teach your child the view of the Scriptures, which is Christ as Lord of all creation, without distinction between sacred and secular.

In the biblical perspective, God's design is to use Christians to restore the broken world in all of its parts, including individuals, nations, the environment, and institutions. This is so important to the biblical understanding of the world and Christian mission that it is the main point of emphasis every year at the CCO's Jubilee Conference. We bring speakers from all over the world to help students bridge any gap in understanding about their living out their faith in church and living it out in their work.

As an example of how a college student might come to integrate a big view of God with a vocation, with sacred and secular being all the same, I share this explanation from Cora, who recently graduated from Ohio Wesleyan University:

> When I tell people I am double majoring in zoology and religion, the response I usually get is, "What are you going to do with that? Minister to the animals?" I always go on to explain that even though it seems like an odd combination, I believe that they work really well together.

When I look around at the world I see evidence for a Creator everywhere. When I take science classes and learn about physiology and ecosystems and organisms I see the fingerprints of God. When I interned at the St. Louis Zoo I observed animals that are fearfully and wonderfully made. When I learn about conservation efforts I believe that the Lord is also passionate about caring for the planet.

The CCO and especially the Jubilee conference have been significant in helping me realize that science and faith do not need to be separate spheres of thought. I have come to realize that my love of science matters to God—that in fact he created me to be passionate about animals and has placed that desire and that call in me. There is no place where this is better discussed than at Jubilee.

The Challenge of Academic Hostility toward Christianity: Prepare by Being Cautious

When conducting my focus group research, I was surprised by the number of incidents of open hostility on the part of faculty to the Christian faith. It is not usually as blatant as "I am here to undo everything your family and your church have taught you," as was the case in one religion department, but I hear variations on this kind of approach. I was also caught off guard by the response of parents, who have seen enough of this that they are generally nonplussed when it happens to their child—they more or less expect it.

Here are a couple of caveats to the hostile professor. First, even as such men and women are more common, they are still a single-digit minority on most faculties. Second, there is a difference between a professor who wants honest dialogue and will push students to defend what they believe and professors who are bullies.

I am going to recommend something here that may meet with considerable disagreement: unless your son or daughter knows his or her stuff, loves to debate, and has a great support system, steer your child clear of the philosophy and religion departments at most schools (Christian colleges and universities being notable exceptions).

My friend Steve, reflecting on his experience in the religion department at a large state school, said, "An Islamic guy taught Islam, a Buddhist Buddhism, and Rabbi Judaism. Bible was taught by someone completely alienated from the Christian faith."

Philosophy classes can be great for the right students (and you'll meet one in a moment), but again, there is a strong possibility that a philosophy professor will work at disassembling the faith of undergraduates.

That said, I'm not suggesting Christian college kids or adults put their heads in the sand academically and fear all debate that challenges faith. I'm simply suggesting that it might not be a good idea to deliberately enter a semester-long situation where someone with grading power and an educational level much higher than your child's tries to destroy your child's faith.

On the other hand, Christians should be people of intellectual curiosity and integrity. If God is in all things, we need not fear those who in any profession or intellectual discipline are hostile. It's important that Christian children learn that a good portion of history's best architects, scientists, philosophers, and musicians did their work as praise to God. When as a parent you model intellectual curiosity and integrity as a Christian, you do your child a genuine favor. This is an antidote to the threats of dualism as well as to being blindsided by intellectual hostility.

Dozens of books, podcasts, and DVDs are available to help you and your child prepare for the intellectually active college environment. Our kids have benefited from going through Focus on the Family's "True U" curriculum, which is designed particularly for high school students who are likely headed for college. For an adult wanting to escape the trap of dualism, I like Nancy Pearcey's book, *Total Truth*. The primer on Christian worldview is Albert Wolters's classic (short) book *Creation Regained*.

Want more resources? Contact my friend Byron Borger at Hearts & Minds books in Dallastown, Pennsylvania, and he will guide you to the latest and greatest. Byron has forgotten more great books than I will ever know.

Christian students *can* thrive in college, even in the face of hostility. Billy Riley's story is a great example. Here it is in Billy's own words:

> As I approached high school graduation, I received stern warnings about the dangers of higher education, liberal professors, and indoctrination, especially around the issue of evolution. While well-meaning, I eventually learned that these attitudes were not the most helpful for me to bring into the college classroom.
>
> Despite limited involvement outside of church in high school, I knew I needed to get involved in whatever Christian presence there was at Washington & Jefferson College (W&J). Within the first few weeks, I connected to the CCO staff at W&J and committed to a small group along with several other freshmen.
>
> With encouragement from this group and because of a new perspective on my education and the learning process, I decided to take a class called Human Origins for my January term. I knew this class was challenging and dealt with the relationship between Christianity and evolution. I didn't know, however, where the professor, Dr. Malinack, would be coming from.
>
> The class was challenging academically, but also spiritually and intellectually. My favorite part, though, ended up being my relationship with Dr. Malinack. A self-described atheist-leaning agnostic, he tried his best to be fair, but inevitably his biases came through.
>
> Although this could be seen as detrimental in a classroom, it ended up providing an opening for me to express the questions and concerns I was dealing with as the course progressed. In papers, I would write about experiences praying about the material, and I stayed after virtually every class, either to barrage the professor with questions or to simply get to know him. As we learned one another's stories and developed a classroom rapport (even giving each other nicknames, Sunday School Billy and Dr. Disclaimer),

the atmosphere moved from possibly threatening to academically and even spiritually stimulating.

I could talk all day about what I learned in that class, but suffice it to say that I am still a Christian. Indeed, because of that class I love Jesus even more deeply. I have a more robust understanding of my faith, of Scripture, and of myself. I learned what can happen when you let a passion for learning, curiosity, and faith rule over attitudes of fear and cynicism.

The following year, Dr, Malinack asked me to be a mentor for one of his freshman classes. And the following January the ministry I was a part of hosted a panel discussion about God's existence, featuring Dr. Malinack and three others. All of this was possible because of my relationship with the professor and because I was secure and supported enough to engage in the classroom rather than put up walls and feel attacked. My experience in Human Origins set the tone for the rest of my career at W&J and led to remarkable experiences inside and outside of the classroom.

Billy Riley graduated from Washington and Jefferson College in 2013 with a dual degree in philosophy and psychology and now works for the CCO at an automotive trade school in western Pennsylvania. The panel discussion Billy describes was called by one professor "the best thing to hit W&J in twenty years." His Human Origins professor, Dr. Steve Malinack, is supportive of Billy and continues to invite Christians to help teach his class.

I DO BELIEVE

My friend Gail Jones came home on a college break in the 1960s and announced to her father, a pastor, that she no longer believed in God. He listened respectfully and calmly to his daughter's perspective and invited her into his study to continue the conversation. He then asked, "Would you like to hear some reasons why I do believe?" Gail doesn't remember that much about Reverend Nesbitt's points, but she does remember leaving the office thinking, "I think I *do* believe!"

The Challenge of Wild Oats, Wild Parties, and Hookup Dangers: Prepare by Having a Conversation with Your Child

In chapter 3, we learned that, contrary to popular belief, kids do *not* have to sow wild oats to have a great college experience. That might be a good thing to ask your kids about before they get to campus.

Do you remember the advice about moving along a continuum from control to conversation in chapter 5? Christian Smith recommends we become conversation partners with our teenagers. I maintain that one of the best ways to do this is to ask questions and listen respectfully.

Here is an example related to alcohol:

Nick, there are generally two ways Christians handle the issue of alcohol: they abstain from it altogether or they enjoy it in moderation. You've seen your mom and me drink a glass of wine or have a beer. Which of these do you imagine you will want to do as an adult: abstain completely or enjoy moderately? Why? What have you heard about college students and drinking? What do you imagine the biggest challenges will be in college relative to alcohol? Any idea how you would like to handle those challenges—especially in sexually charged situations?

For a girl, the conversation would look very similar, but I would be inclined to more directly visit the link between excess drinking, sexual activity, and sexual violence.

Jennifer, I don't want to freak you out, but I need to ask: What do you know about the relationship between drinking and sexual regrets and sexual violence during college? Have you heard or read anything?

Questions form the transition to a back-and-forth discussion about a sensitive but important topic for young women. It can broaden to other safety-related issues for them, like walking across campus alone at night.

I recommend allowing the teenager/college student to declare himself or herself. What does the teenager really want his or her college experience to be like? What are your child's ideas about the problems Christian students face in college? Follow a principle of leadership: people will work a lot harder to achieve their goals than they will your goals.

Here is what the conversation might sound like with regard to opposition to the faith—active or passive—on campus:

> Tiffany, the other day I was thinking about what's ahead of you . . . you know, probably going away to college, and I thought of some things I've seen and read about. They have to do with college professors or others who don't believe as you do—lots of people are in that category—but some are pretty vocal, maybe even aggressive, toward Christians and the Christian faith. Have you heard about that at all from any of your older friends or your brothers? Have you had experiences like that in high school? What was it like? How do you imagine you would respond if a professor went after you or your faith? Or if a fellow student was an atheist and wanted to tell you why your faith was stupid—how do you imagine you would want to respond?

I'd like to highlight two parts of these questions and the conversation they would invite. First, I try to keep the ball in the child's court. There may be a time and place for more directive language ("Here's what to do when a professor comes after you, Tiffany"), but we lead more effectively when we ask more of our followers. The challenge will ultimately be the child's, not ours, so allowing the child to wrestle with the question rather than us spoon-feeding the answer is the preferred way to go.

Second, notice that you are giving your child a chance to think about something before it happens. Not only is the child thinking about it, but he or she is starting to actually rehearse it. Rehearsal is a beautiful thing, as it makes the actual moment of truth (the performance) a whole lot easier and a whole lot more fun.

If the conversation is really going well, and your child is open to it, you can actually try role-playing. "I'll be the college junior trying to ply you with alcohol and you be . . . you." "You be the professor and I'll be the student. Be nice to me—I haven't been in school for a long time!" Role-playing takes rehearsal to yet another level.

Final Words on Thriving

In the testimonies in this chapter, you will notice a consistency: each student is involved in campus ministry. For Ris, Gabi, Jeff, and Jacob, being plugged into a ministry helped their understanding of God and his work in the world (and in them) grow by leaps and bounds.

In Billy's case, campus ministry connection was key to answering the challenges inherent in the Human Origins class.

As we considered your influence in chapter 6 and the place of peer influence in chapter 8, we talked about the two unsolicited pieces of advice worth giving to a child on the cusp of college: go to church and get involved in a weekly campus fellowship of some kind.

If thriving is the goal, connection to other Christians, exposure to scriptural teaching, and going deeper into the gospel are musts for your son or daughter during college. This is true even for kids attending a Christian school, where many students end up going with the flow when they could open in full blossom.

So here is one last conversation, rehearsed.

Beth, I'm excited about what's ahead at Big State U. Your mom and I have tried to stay away from giving you a bunch of unsolicited advice. But I want to ask two things of you while you are at college—they are both really important, but it will be up to you to decide if you want to do them. I would like you to go to church and be part of a weekly fellowship meeting of some kind on campus. I picture a church where you can continue to learn about the Scriptures and find a way to serve, and a fellowship that could be anything from a gathering of hundreds to a Bible study on your dorm floor. Can you sort of picture both those things: the church and the fellowship?

It will be your choice, of course. You will decide if you do either of these things or both. I can't make you do them, and I'll be miles away when you are doing them or not doing them. The only thing you need to know is that your mom and I will ask you about church and fellowship periodically. Does that make sense?

10

When the Wheels Are Falling Off

Look for Spiritual Growth

"Consider it pure joy, my brothers and sisters, whenever you face trials of many kinds, because you know that the testing of your faith produces perseverance" (James 1:2–3).

Author's Note: Are you kidding me?

When have you been most alive in your faith?

I asked the parents in my Youngstown, Ohio, focus group to put this question to their kids. The answer from one college student, John, caught me off guard: "I felt most alive in my faith when I was fifteen and lost my best friend to leukemia." How could something so devastating leave a young man feeling "alive in his faith"?

How about this question: *What helped prepare you to be a faithful Christian in college?*

Heather, a senior at Wheaton College, gave this answer to her parents: "When Dad lost his job and we had to move to a different state during the summer before my senior year in high school." She described this as the time when her "world was crushed."

As a dad, I can think of few things more difficult than watching one of our kids suffer. Cutting remarks from a friend, failure in school, and getting cut from an athletic team are all part of growing up. Still, these experiences are not all that much different on the pain barometer than broken bones.

If I hadn't heard it directly from the kids themselves, I never, ever would have imagined that painful experiences were an important theme in preparing to own a personal and vibrant faith.

Parents, Kids, and Pain

We are never more pain-averse than in our roles as Mom or Dad. As the saying goes, "Once you become a parent, you will never be any happier than your unhappiest child." Isn't it so?

Whatever distaste we may have personally for suffering, trials, and the like, our desire to see our kids avoid pain is exponentially larger. I have a fear of heights, but I didn't know what fear really was until I saw our playful, derring-do, fifteen-year-old sons get close to the edge of a two-hundred-foot drop on a trip through the Rocky Mountains.

If we consider objectively what causes human beings to develop courage, patience, empathy, or most any other virtue, it's hard to avoid the obvious: men and women grow the most through adversity. For the Christian, suffering is also a means of better knowing God. "I want to know Christ—yes, to know the power of his resurrection and participation in his sufferings" (Phil. 3:10).

And yet we don't readily see this with our kids, precisely because of our role as their protectors. Keeping our children safe is a good, God-ordained parental responsibility, but it can become more than that, particularly in our day. Parents, many whose lives are testimonies to "whatever doesn't kill you makes you stronger," will go to extremes to keep their kids from life's bumps and bruises.

But that is not how God grows human beings into something beautiful. He uses the hard stuff.

A Culture of (Dis)Ease

Many years ago, when I worked for the CCO at Penn State, an engineering student shared this with me: "My parents want me to get a good job and not throw too many years of income away on renting. They think I should own a house soon."

Two questions naturally followed: "What was your parents' experience like when they first started out?" and "How do they feel about that experience now?"

Almost universally, moms and dads who, reflecting back, report barely having had two nickels to rub together, living as renters in humble circumstances (how about in a funeral home?), and generally doing without are not bitter. In fact, they look back fondly on the relative "hardship" of having little and figuring out how to navigate life together.

It's natural to want our kids to do better than we did and to have what we didn't have, but is that always such a good thing? Our culture says in a thousand ways, "Yes!" But this encourages us and our kids to be consumers and accumulators—that is, people who judge the quality of life by possessions and comfort.

The antidote to this kind of thinking is to consider the potential benefit of discomfort from God's point of view. First, let's take a look at how people, particularly religious people, view suffering.

How Religious People View Suffering

Nowhere save the sufferings of Jesus Christ himself is suffering more obvious than in the biblical character Job. He loses his children, a good portion of his fortune, and finally his health. He devolves from a rich man who loves God and has great dignity to a wreck sitting on an ash heap scratching his boils with broken pieces of pottery. His own wife finally tells him to "curse God and die!" (Job 2:9).

But at least Job has friends. Or does he? Four buddies come to comfort him. One by one the friends explain to Job that his suffering is linked to some prior sin Job has committed. This conversation is lengthy and at no point does anyone guess the truth—that Job's predicament was caused by a deal between God and the devil (see Job 1:6–12).

Like good religious people, Job's friends think of his immense misfortune in cause-and-effect terms. "You have done something wrong and so God is punishing you." Isn't this the way things work in a moral universe?

Job is a very old book, but this thinking was alive and well in Jesus's day. "There were some present at that very time who told him about the Galileans whose blood Pilate had mingled with their sacrifices. And he answered them, 'Do you think that these Galileans were worse sinners than all the other Galileans, because they suffered in this way? No, I tell you; but unless you repent, you will all likewise perish. Or those eighteen on whom the tower in Siloam fell and killed them: do you think that they were worse offenders than all the others who lived in Jerusalem? No, I tell you; but unless you repent, you will all likewise perish'" (Luke 13:1–5 ESV).

In another scene, Jesus and his followers encounter a blind man. "His disciples asked him, 'Rabbi, who sinned, this man or his parents, that he was born blind?' 'Neither this man nor his parents sinned,' said Jesus, 'but this happened so that the works of God might be displayed in him'" (John 9:2–3).

Jesus hears the scuttlebutt about some fellow Galileans who met a horrible end. Chiming in, Jesus adds another disaster that took the lives of eighteen people who were crushed by a tower that fell in Jerusalem. He opens the eyes of not only a blind man but also the disciples, as they assume the man's affliction comes from something he or his parents did wrong. Jesus knows the subtext because he knows how we religious types think. Those who lost their lives or their sight through humanly, inexplicable circumstances must have had it coming.

In Job's case, God answers the question of the religious with his own questions, such as, "Where were you when I laid the earth's foundation?" (Job 38:4). Jesus likewise reframes the whole conversation by reminding his hearers that all human beings are part of our race's insurrection against our Creator and therefore eligible for punishment. Were the victims worse than you? No! Perhaps someone's suffering is merely a prelude to a great work of God's healing, as in the case of the blind man.

If you are a Christian parent who wants more than anything to see your child walk through life hand in hand with Jesus, then you—like me—are to some degree a "religious type." We often make the mistake of thinking we are better than those bad Pharisees with whom Jesus seems in perpetual conflict. It would be more helpful to us in our relationship to our kids to understand ourselves as described by writer John Fischer: recovering Pharisees.[1] We are fully capable of every self-righteous thought, judgmental comment, angry outburst we see from religious people who fight with our Lord on the pages of Scripture.

How God Views Suffering

God allows hard things into the lives of his well-loved children so we can become the people he wants us to be. As I am reminded by the passages below, he uses trials, hardships, and outright suffering to build our character and deepen our faith. What is true for us is true for our children. Perhaps inserting your children's name(s) into these passages will help you shift to a different perspective. I will put my name in first, because I am addicted to comfort and still see suffering as a negative, completely undesirable phenomenon.

Consider it pure joy . . . whenever [Dan] face[s] trials of many kinds, because you know that the testing of [his] faith produces perseverance. Let perseverance finish its work that [Dan] may be mature and complete, not lacking anything. (James 1:2–4)

Not only so, but we also glory in [Dan's] sufferings, because suffering produces perseverance; perseverance, character; and character, hope. And hope does not put [Dan] to shame, because God's love has been poured out into [Dan's heart] through the Holy Spirit, who has been given to [him]. (Rom. 5:3–5)

I consider that [Dan's] present sufferings are not worth comparing with the glory that will be revealed in [him]. (Rom. 8:18)

How to Help Our Children Walk through Suffering

Suffering begins early, even for kids who do not have to deal with life-threatening illnesses, injuries, or debilitating conditions that bring daily pain. Small children are *suffering machines*—producing enough head bonks, scraped knees, and smashed fingers in one day to put any adult to shame.

I saw how my wife handled these, using steps she learned from other women:

1. Stop the action and acknowledge the hurt.
2. Pray with the child, asking for God's help to bring healing and help the pain be less (enduring suffering does not mean passive resignation; we want our kids to ask for help early and often).
3. Apply soap and water, Band-Aids, gauze, or ice as appropriate.
4. Call the doctor if necessary.

If you are thinking, "That's not exactly rocket science," you are right! Parenting, like anything else, is not all that complicated when sectioned into smaller parts. Profound ideas matter less than the consistent practice of simple steps. Notice what a child can learn through many, many "owies" over the years:

1. Your mom or dad will walk with you through your suffering.
2. God cares when you scrape your knee. He will also walk through your suffering with you and is able to do something about it.
3. Turning to God and praying for help is not the enemy of taking action (e.g., putting on a Band-Aid or applying some ice).

As our kids get bigger and run into fewer pieces of furniture, they encounter troubles of a whole different kind. You've heard the adage: *Little people have little problems, big people have big problems.* The wounds left by bigger problems, especially the kind in the social arena, are often invisible, but they can hurt a lot more. The wound might involve a deserting friend or an adult who tells your child he or she will never amount to anything.

Job's four friends, Elihu, Bildad, Zophar, and Eliphaz, set the example of what not to do. *It is a bad idea to tell your kid or anyone else why he or she is suffering.* No matter your intent, it will usually come across as unloving and presumptuous. The exceptions are young children (your brother gave you a bloody nose because you called him a fathead) and adults who are asking for diagnostic help. Even in such cases, tread carefully, as many of us may ask a friend, "Why is this happening to me?" not because we are looking for a direct answer, but because we are crying out in our pain.

A beautiful verse from Paul's Galatian letter instructs us in responding to our children's suffering, particularly as they get older. "Bear one another's burdens and so fulfill the law of Christ" (Gal. 6:2 ESV). Two ways to do that are listening and reminding.

Listening. We bear our kids' burdens in these circumstances by listening without judgment, praying, and filling the hearts and minds of our kids with God's Word. I've not been entirely fair to Job's friends on this count, who before they begin to tell him why his life is horrible, actually sit with Job in silence for several days. "Listening" may be an exercise in merely offering your physical presence as your son or daughter cries. Eventually, words will come. As they do, you will have to resist the temptation to offer a solution to the problem. Though it may seem abundantly clear to you why this suffering is occurring, hold back, even if it means stuffing a sock in your mouth! If you must speak, repeat what you hear your child saying in your own words (called active listening), or better yet, ask your child if you may pray for him or her.

Reminding. Instead of trying to answer the unanswerable, when it is finally time to talk, remind your child of what he or she already knows: both God and you love your child. Encourage your child to bring whatever he or she is feeling in their gut directly to God, even if it is ugly. It helps here if your child is acquainted with Scripture, particularly the psalms, which are sometimes so raw with emotion that they seem out of bounds for religious, God-fearing people.

> Why, LORD, do you stand far off?
>> Why do you hide yourself in times of trouble?
>>> (Ps. 10:1)

> My God, my God, why have you forsaken me?
>> Why are you so far from saving me, from the words of
>> my groaning? (Ps. 22:1 ESV)

> I say to God my Rock,
>> "Why have you forgotten me?
> Why must I go about mourning,
>> oppressed by the enemy?" (Ps. 42:9)

> Awake, LORD! Why do you sleep?
>> Rouse yourself! Do not reject us forever.
> Why do you hide your face
>> and forget our misery and oppression? (Ps. 44:23–24)

164

O God, why have you rejected us forever?
  Why does your anger smolder against the sheep of your
    pasture? (Ps. 74:1)

Why do you hold back your hand, your right hand?
  Take it from the folds of your garment and destroy
    them! (Ps. 74:11)

Obviously, staying mad at God or other people is not healthy for our children or us. Appropriate confession of how we really feel actually interrupts our tendency toward bitterness. "God, it feels like you have abandoned me" (see Ps. 74:11) is not a bad place to start.

Then There Is Jesus

Jesus suffered more than any human ever has. When Mel Gibson produced the film *The Passion of the Christ*, many viewers were offended by the amount of blood shown on-screen. But the scourging with a whip and the crucifixion itself were bloody, awful experiences. By all accounts, hanging on a cross is a particularly cruel way to die—slow, agonizing, and humiliating.

The deeper pain—which no other human can or will ever experience—was that of enduring separation from God the Father to whom he had been joined in love from all eternity. On the cross, Jesus is forgotten. From this pit of abandonment he repeats the words of the psalmist: "My God, my God, why have you forsaken me?" (Matt. 27:46).

Jesus was forsaken in our place, undone and forgotten, that we could be remade and remembered. Yes, he has suffered what we have in every way and then some. Our kids need to know that God can understand their pain, not just in theory, but by virtue of his own experience.

Jesus, therefore, is uniquely qualified to utter these words: "Come to me, all you who are weary and burdened, and I will give you rest. Take my yoke upon you and learn from me, for I am gentle and humble in heart, and you will find rest for your souls. For my yoke is easy and my burden is light" (Matt. 11:28–30). It's not just that Jesus can relate to our troubles, but that he is willing to endure them *with us*. This is a gift to give our children, the understanding that God will walk through the deepest valley with them, even where the shadow of death itself hangs over them.

Remember the young man I quoted at the beginning of the chapter, John, who found himself alive in faith in the midst of his worst nightmare, the death of a friend? His faith was deepened because Jesus was there to meet him at his deepest point of grief. When Heather described the impact of leaving home and friends right before her senior year in high school, it sounded like this: "I think a lot of (high school) seniors are still 'on top of the world' and go into college with that attitude. It makes it harder to follow Christ when you have never really had a point in your life when he is all you had." Heather learned to lean into God and his promises because she had no other viable choice. Her faith in Jesus became the most important reality in her life, and she learned that she could trust him, even in circumstances she would never choose.

Daily Parenting Practices to Remember

Don't overprotect. In 2001, my hometown, Cincinnati, suffered through four days of race riots, begun by the shooting of a twenty-seven-year-old African-American man on a hot August night. A year later, the CCO cosponsored an event with John Perkins, one of the fathers of the racial reconciliation movement. At the core of Perkins's worldview is the idea of inherent human dignity. Here is what he said at the event: "People have been asking me to come to Cincinnati for a year, but I waited, because I think people should have the privilege of solving their own problems."

I don't generally think of undoing my own mess as a privilege.

There is an unseen cost of overprotecting our kids, of solving their problems for them, even when they are at an age when they are able to do so themselves. We take away the opportunity for their dignity to grow. A kid who has dignity is a confident kid—he or she has a center of gravity that Martin Luther King Jr. called "somebodyness."

When I conducted my focus groups with parents, I noticed an interesting pattern. Parents whose children were thriving the most in college and beyond had allowed their kids some bumps and bruises during high school. They had given them "rope" to create and solve some of their own problems.

Talk about suffering, trials, and consequences. I recently heard a professor trace the glorious presence of God from the Old Testament to the New Testament. Where is the glory of God most evident in the Bible and the life of the church? When we are fragile and cracked, because "we have this treasure [God's light] in jars of clay to show that this all-surpassing power is from God and not from us" (2 Cor. 4:7).

From early on we have the opportunity to talk with our kids about how God can and will use trials. Find a way to talk about the hard side of life with your kids. Give them some Scripture and maybe a story or two that illustrate the distinctly Christian point of view on the topic.

Don't pretend. Years ago Huey Lewis had a song with the lyric, "Sometimes, bad is bad." Though he meant something a bit different, the concept pertains to life's difficulties. Ignoring pain or stoically adopting a "no regrets" policy may seem like a good idea in the short run, but that pain will find a way to express itself in surprising and unwelcome ways. Let your kids see you walk through the hard places with grace, but also with honesty.

Ask for help. There is a difference between a healthy journey into suffering and clinical depression. If your child is so blue that he or she can't get out of bed, is cutting, not eating, abusing alcohol or drugs, acting out sexually, flying into rages, or manifesting behavior that could hurt him or herself or others, get a recommendation for a Christian counselor and make an appointment.

Have the cause-doesn't-equal-effect conversation. As our walk through Job and subsequent visit with Jesus showed, religious people have a tendency to assume a hurting person did something to earn his or her misery. A risk of growing up in the church is that your kids will catch a "they must have had it coming" attitude toward the suffering of others. Look for an opportunity to speak to the "Why?" of human suffering—help your kids learn not to assume the worst of others or themselves. Consider giving them an experience similar to Sarah's trip to India (see chap. 7), which exposed her to suffering people on a much bigger scale.

Have the cause-does-equal-effect conversation. Some of the suffering our kids will experience, of course, will be the result of their own impulsive or wayward actions. It's our job to help them distinguish between what is not their fault (death of a friend, failing when they try hard) and what is a natural outcome of their poor choices.

Start conversations about actions and consequences early. "If you hit Johnny, he might hit you back." Encourage your child to think through specific actions and discover what the consequences might be. "So, Jeffrey, if you and your teammates stay up all night at an overnighter before your Saturday morning basketball game, what might happen to you and your teammates as the game goes on?" Keep the conversations going, particularly if you have an adolescent at home whose desire for adventure might occasionally run ahead of his or her common sense. In most cases, there is no need to be a wet blanket—invite your kids to figure more of these things out for themselves as they get older.

When your son or daughter makes a bad choice—even a doozie—consider it a great teaching opportunity. Walk your child through repentance, and help him or her understand that God loves and forgives even when a person is experiencing some nasty consequences. The promises of refinement through trials are directed to

God's people, young and old: "All things work together for good, for those who are called according to his purpose" (Rom. 8:28 ESV).

From early on we can help our kids understand the biblical narrative of sin, repentance, and restoration. It will help if they are steeped in the gospel stories of restoration: David after Bathsheba and Uriah (see 2 Sam. 11; Ps. 51); Peter after denying Jesus three times (see Luke 22:54–60; John 21:15–22).

Perhaps more than by any of the other findings in the research I've done to write this book, I've been brought up short by how God uses hard things to mature our kids. I will always feel pain when one of my kids does, but I have a fresh perspective about how God can use that pain in my child's life. Rather than pray for my children to be spared any pain at all, which was never realistic, I now pray for God to do his full work in any circumstance. I am more intentional in the conversations I have about pain and suffering with my kids.

I may never get completely used to the idea that, in God's loving economy, pain is an opportunity for growth. I will, however, cling to this biblical promise to me, you, and all of our kids: "Neither death nor life, neither angels nor demons, neither the present nor the future, nor any powers, neither height nor depth, nor anything else in all creation, will be able to separate us from the love of God that is in Christ Jesus our Lord" (Rom. 8:38–39).

11

The Worst Is Happening

It's Not Time to Give Up

Do you remember the story line of the musical *Fiddler on the Roof*? Chava, the third daughter of Tevye the dairyman, falls in love with Chvedka, a young man from the village. Chvedka, unlike Tevye and his family, is a goy, a non-Jew.

Over the protests of her father, Chava and Chvedka get married. In a poignant scene, Chava begs for her father's acceptance. Tevye wrestles with the decision: *Do I reach out to the daughter I love, or do I do what my faith demands (as far as I understand it) and turn my back on her as if she does not exist?* Finally, Tevye, who has already given another daughter away to a Jewish Marxist, concludes, "If I try and bend that far, I'll break." He turns his back on Chava, and she cries in anguish as he walks away. It is a heartbreaking scene of abandonment and rejection.

Children from Christian homes make a variety of choices that fall outside their parents' values. These choices range from living a promiscuous lifestyle, to partying excessively, to marrying someone of questionable character, to choosing a career solely to make piles of money, to walking away from faith and church. These choices can lead to heartbreaking, life-altering outcomes, including alienation from the rest of the family, a life lived apart from God, an unplanned pregnancy, divorce, and chronic unemployment.

So what do we, as Christian parents, do when our children choose to walk away from our Christian values, in small and large ways? What do we do if they walk away from God altogether? Do we, like Tevye, declare that our son or daughter is "dead to me"? Where is the line? What would God have us do?

If you are a parent who struggles with questions like these and the related emotions, you are not alone. Recently I had lunch with a father of three adult children, two of whom do not share the faith so important to him and his wife. The "kids" in question are thirty-seven and forty. Is it time to give up, throw in the towel on matters of faith?

Eighteen months ago the talented, spunky daughter of church friends wondered aloud to her parents if they would still welcome her home for summer break, even if she no longer believed in God.

In a response to an email survey we sent to parents, one said, "Our daughter went to church without prompting, married a Christian man, and is actively involved in their church. Our son walked away from the faith in college, and we are still praying for him."

Feeling Responsible

It's bad enough to see your child choose a life that will be so much less than it could be, but when you feel personally responsible in some way, it's even harder. You might legitimately bear this burden through neglect, abuse, lack of faith, or a poor example. On the other hand, you might have walked faithfully with Jesus and done all you could to help your kids do the same. Chances are the answer is a bit of both, given that we are all broken. No matter what the reality, your child's rejection of the faith or other bad choices will become a weapon in the hands of the Enemy. Count on it. You will feel the sting of darts hurled by the "accuser of our brothers and sisters" (Rev. 12:10).

We need to address the false burden of guilt and shame parents whose kids are not thriving in faith often experience. Carrying this weighty burden is in opposition to what God has for us. It is also counterproductive and senselessly painful. Consider the following:

- As a parent, you are not God and not in control of the universe, let alone the mind and heart of another human being, even if that person happens to be your child. Your emerging adult kids are individuals who do things for their own reasons. They are responsible for their own choices.

- Parenting, even Christian parenting, is messy work with unpredictable results. Even Billy and Ruth Graham had a prodigal son. Ruth Graham announced this to the world with a book. A wayward child is part of the struggle that comes with living in a broken world; it is not an indictment of your character.

- Carrying the weight of guilt over parental missteps or failure will not help you be a better parent in the future. Use your energy to love your son or daughter now. In the present.

- Misplaced guilt and shame often show up in exactly the wrong place. If you feel you must "shun" your child, even unofficially, you may well be reacting out of your own frustration at your perceived failure. There is a good chance the shunning will make things worse. (I'm not talking about healthy boundaries, which are essential.)

- A large theme in our Christian journeys is learning to ask for and receive forgiveness. If we have failed our kids (as we all have), God expects us to repent, not to wallow in guilt. He expects us to go to him, asking for insight regarding the path forward.

• As is often attributed to Winston Churchill: "Never, never, never give up."[1] God's demonstrated pattern is to pursue us when we are far from him. His nature is to love and to woo. I've heard plenty of accounts from men and women who walked away from the Christian faith only to come back twenty, thirty, or even fifty years later.

Let's consider the heart of God on the matter.

Now That Would Make a Good Story

Jesus will ultimately go to the cross to accomplish reconciliation with God on our behalf, but when he wants to explain reconciliation beforehand, he spins the tale of a father and two sons.

The parable of the prodigal son packs a novel's worth of meaning into a story that takes about four minutes to tell (see Luke 15:11–31). The youngest of two sons approaches his father and asks for his portion of the inheritance while his dad is still living. Scholars tell us this behavior is the cultural equivalent of expressing a wish for his father to be dead. In spite of this insult, the dad gives him the money, which the son spends on what one neither writes home nor calls to tell his parents about. The son goes broke, is caught in a famine, and gets a job feeding pigs in a field.

We don't know what the father is doing while all of this is happening, but based on what we see later, he is likely grieved by both his son's rashness and his absence. He would dearly like to see the boy again.

Experts tell us it is important for someone with an addiction to reach a point low enough that he or she utters, like Popeye, "That's all I can stand, I can't stands no more." Getting hungry enough to eat the pods the pigs eat seems to be that point for the son. Finally, he realizes that, having forfeited his right to sonship by his behavior, he can at least attempt to hire on at his dad's house as a servant.

While the son is on his way home, and as Jesus says "a long way off" (v. 20), his father sees him and runs to meet him. The father puts nice clothes on the wayward young adult, gives him a place of honor in the family, and throws a big party.

At this point in the story, we, as parents who have read self-help books, might ask, "Where is the family dignity here? Doesn't that father know his son must be accountable for his actions? How will the young man learn anything if it is so easy to come back? Where is the 'come to Jesus' lecture?"

Actually, there is someone else in the family who has sense enough to ask himself these kinds of questions. The older brother also wonders bitterly what he, who has faithfully served his dad and never run away, must do to have a party he can invite his friends to. Yes, the eldest son reasons like a good religious person should.

The story of the prodigal son is one of outlandish grace in response to despicable and publicly humiliating behavior to a parent. How interesting that God chooses this story to describe his relationship to us! How interesting that it also demonstrates, albeit loosely, good parenting.

As individuals, we respond to the offer of God's outlandish grace in one of two ways: like the younger brother ("Really, I'm not disowned?") or the older ("I'm doing everything right; how come you haven't figured out how wonderful I am?"). Read the parable again and imagine how life will go for each of these boys after the story ends. I suspect the younger fellow will probably give his dad heartburn from time to time, but he will also live life with a deep sense of gratitude. The older has already revealed his true heart toward the father, which is full of contempt. This attitude has been growing in the older brother's heart for a long time. Unless interrupted, it will continue to grow until it completely consumes him and he is no more. That is what unresolved bitterness does.

The parable is not, strictly speaking, meant to be a lesson in parenthood. But are we to draw no conclusions as to how a human family is to function when we ourselves are the prodigal or have a child who is? No, there is plenty for us to learn about parenting as we see God portrayed in the story.

The father never stops loving the son. The father's love is not dependent on the son's actions. The father loves the son no more when he is obedient and no less when he is disobedient. We could question the father's judgment in giving the boy his inheritance, but that's not the central point of the story. We could also say the father needs to be realistic and set boundaries so the betrayal doesn't repeat itself. Again, that's not the point of the story.

When it is time to forgive, the father is so ready that we see him blow right through his son's well-rehearsed mea culpa. To quote Pumba (from *The Lion King*), he puts his "behind in the past" and celebrates getting back the son who was lost.

As I consider that this is how God feels about me, it is beautiful and overwhelming and humbling. It's unbelievable and at the same time it is more true than anything else in the universe, except God himself. God celebrates because I was lost and now am found, as he celebrates if you have also turned and headed for home.

Here is what we see in the father in the parable: God's forgiveness. This is our supply, our deep reservoir that is always there when we need to forgive others. We will need to draw from this supply if we are to love the prodigals in our families. As God has done with you, you are now free to do with your lost child. I'm not suggesting it's easy!

Forgiven. Now What?

In chapter 1, I told you the story of two families whose parents sat around a dining room table with me in suburban Philadelphia, surrounded by several other parents. You remember the scenario: one couple with five kids who had by and large stayed out of trouble, and another with two kids, one of whom was living with her boyfriend and the other whose girlfriend had become pregnant. Of course, the second family had the "What should we have done differently?" conversation, but beyond that, there was this reality: "We are now grandparents in a way we never hoped for."

So what do we do when our son or daughter goes off "to a distant country," whatever that may be? I can't claim to have personal experience here, but I've learned a great deal from Scripture, experts, and parents.

I've learned that most kids do not need constant reminders of their failure—they know when they have made a mess of things and may struggle to remain hopeful. By law of the universe, these kids will experience the consequences of their choices, and browbeating them is neither necessary nor helpful. I remember once housebreaking a puppy by sticking its nose near its stool and whacking it on the nose with a rolled-up newspaper. Your derailed son or daughter is likely in daily contact with his or her mess, and stuffing their nose in it and meting out punishments is probably not the antidote. Apparently this method is not even effective for puppies!

Consider Options, Choices, and Your Marriage

The best moves to make when your child gets derailed depend to a large degree in how your child is squaring up to his or her choices and the outcomes of those choices. If your daughter, for instance, owns what she has done, wants to chart a different and better course, and is responsive to the counsel of others, you will be able to find many ways to help. Keep the ball in her court as much as possible—allowing her the dignity of facing and dealing with her own problems. Be a willing helper as much as you can, knowing that you may have to periodically shoulder more of the load than you would like. You will have to judge your child's capacity to deal with the mess she is in.

If your child is unwilling to name the real issue ("I cannot control my use of drugs and alcohol"), consistently minimizes the issue's seriousness, or externalizes his choices (also known as blame-shifting), the road back to restoration may be a long one.

In some cases, the journey may take place over decades. You may have to draw boundaries where you never dreamed they would be—asking your adult child to move out of your home, refusing financial support, and/or limiting the amount of contact you have. These are hard, hard moments for parents. You may need to soberly consider what might happen if you don't put some tough boundaries in place.

Here is the story of my own first family, based not on the disobedience of a child (that would have been my story) but on the challenges that came with the mental illness of my oldest sister.

My sister Deb was going on eighteen when I was born. She was a talented, bright child with a wonderful future. During her adolescent years, though, Deb suffered the onset of severe epilepsy. It is hard to describe how frightening a grand mal epileptic seizure is if you have never witnessed one. For a time, Deb was having multiple seizures every day. I can only imagine what this was like for my brother, Dave, and my sister Dougie, and especially Mom and Dad. Mom confesses in her memoir that she (Mom) would go to sleep some nights hoping that she didn't wake up the next day. Mom was not one to throw in the towel (or let any of us throw it in), so she was living close to the abyss at this point.

My parents did everything they could for Deb, who somehow through her own resilient, hopeful outlook and the love of her family made it all the way through college and for a time held down a job. Through a neurosurgeon friend of the family, Deb was able to have two brain surgeries at the National Institutes of Health (NIH) and was afforded the latest in antiseizure medication. This was still in the 1950s and early 1960s, though, and the medication turned out to have a significant side effect: schizophrenia.

The combination of violent, life-threatening seizures and schizophrenic behavior (which could also include violence) made it dangerous for Deb to live on her own and made our home a scary place when she was with us. I remember coming home from elementary school to find our kitchen with a broken sliding glass window and other signs of destruction. To this day, I don't know if Deb had an angry outburst or a seizure, but I remember recognizing that something awful was happening at 134 Lafayette Lane.

Thus began a long journey of my parents helping Deb find a place where she would be safe. This included a state mental institution, at least one halfway house, an apartment next to a day treatment facility, and, in her last decade, the Stewart Home School in Kentucky. When Deb died from a brain tumor at the age of sixty-four, she was more at peace than at any time in my living memory. She lived in a community where she had good boundaries, someone to monitor her medication, and an opportunity to contribute to the well-being of others. She had also become part of a Bible study and seemed to be in an entirely different place with God than had been the case throughout her adult life. I will always admire how my parents loved Deb and provided for her within the constraints and resources available to them.

The mental illness of a child is often too much for a marriage to handle—different studies show a variety of outcomes, but the parents of children with mental illness and addiction split up at a much higher rate than the general population. My parents took many heroic steps during my sister's life, including beginning a business to help pay for her medical expenses.

From the perspective of the youngest child, though, their most valiant deed was staying married. They made it all the way to the finish line when my father passed away at age ninety-two. Sixty-seven years of marriage.

When you weigh options related to your child's destructive choices or a condition (which they may not have chosen), consider the wear and tear on your marriage. It is not easy to consign a youngster to a boarding school as a teen or a treatment facility as a college student, but be honest with each other about how the stress of dealing with your child's problems is affecting you and how you see it affecting your spouse and other children. Allow men and women into your life who can call it like they see it with regard to your marriage. Get as much professional help as you need.

Let Your Marriage Be a Covering

In traditional Jewish weddings, couples get married under a cloth, floral, or similar canopy, which symbolizes the formation of a home together. Called a chuppah (or huppah or chuppa), this canopy is a picture of beauty and—I believe—safety. For kids, our marriages should be their earthly chuppah. It is as if Mom and Dad's promised love and fidelity is a covering under which life is fundamentally safe. This applies not only to small children but to twenty- and thirty-somethings.

Though your child's crisis may demand an immediate, full-on response, delayed launches into independence, or just a whole lot of prayer and patience, you will be most helpful if you can work through this without blowing up your marriage. So, husbands and wives, give each other some time and attention, communicate frequently (more often when things are bad), listen well, stay connected to your friends, and get the help of a Christian counselor if you feel stuck.

When Kids Are Managing Life without God

In matters of faith, cataclysmic events aren't the most typical source of heartbreak for parents. The most persistent pain often comes when a child grows up to find they can do life without God. Let's imagine your nonbelieving adult child is kind, hardworking, well adjusted, and, dare we say, happy. All without God. You may ask yourself, "If my son can have such a good life outside of faith and the church, why should I worry about him or keep pestering him to get to church?"

I think of churchgoing friends whose daughter and son-in-law are raising three beautiful children, holding down two good jobs, serving others in the community, and enjoying life. There may be "God-shaped holes" in their daughter's and son-in-law's hearts, but those holes seem comfortable right now.

The Sixty-Seven-Year-Old Prodigal

Again, the admonition is, "Don't give up." Vern Bengston, a member of the faculty at the University of Southern California, was a self-described prodigal with little chance of return. The only one of nine children and thirty-three cousins who walked away from his faith, Bengston's erosion of belief coincided with the completion of a master's degree and a PhD. As he saw his own faith wane while everyone else in his family believed, he wondered how families passed on faith, and why it is that some children believe and others don't. The Bengstons can trace evangelical Christian faith in their family all the way back to at least the sixteenth century. That's five hundred years or so of baton passing!

Bengston's wondering became his field of research. Beginning in 1970, Dr. Bengston and his team studied 350 families across thirty-five years to understand how faith-passing works. The result was his book *Families and Faith: How Religion Is Passed Down across Generations.*

Still, Bengston himself was an example of a faith not passed on. For years his mother prayed for him and continued to make the case, mainly through her own life, for following Jesus.

Here is what happened to Vern Bengston at age sixty-seven, several decades after he left for a "distant country":

> I woke one Sunday morning missing choir music. As I walked in the door of a massive Gothic church in downtown Santa Barbara, the choir was roaring away and the congregation was shouting praise. Light from the stained glass windows filtered down on the congregation and reflected back up into the great barrel-vaulted ceiling. I was overcome by emotion. To borrow the language of C. S. Lewis, I was "surprised by joy," and I haven't been the same

since. That was a religious reawakening in which, after 65 years of searching, I found a faith community that meant something to me profoundly. Prodigals can come home.[2]

Dr. Bengston wishes his mom was still alive to see his return. The prospect of dying before seeing a prodigal come home may not fit into an ideal happy ending, but this story shouts, "Never, never, never give up!" To quote another praying mom (and grandmother), "The story isn't over yet."

Leaning on God's Promises

When a crash landing happens, our kids need to know one thing above everything else: we still love them. We may struggle with our own anger, resentment, regret, or self-doubt, but we need to struggle with God and get the support of our own friends so we can love our kids the way God has loved us.

Consider these words of Paul expressing his belief about his beloved family, his children in the Lord: "In all my prayers for all of you, I always pray with joy because of your partnership in the gospel from the first day until now, being confident of this, that he who began a good work in you will carry it on to completion until the day of Christ Jesus" (Phil. 1:4–6).

This is one of many good promises to grab hold of prayerfully for your child, whether he or she is walking with or away from Jesus. God started this whole project, not you. If you love him, it is because he first loved you. You were not saved by your efforts at righteous living but by Jesus's sacrifice on your behalf.

You may be the most fertile couple on the planet, but you did not have the power to conceive a child, nor form one in the womb, knitting together chromosomes into a human being. You may have shared the good news of Christ's love and seen your child respond at an early age, but remember in the awe of the moment how sure you were that this was God's work and not yours?

God intends to finish the work he began with your child. The project will probably not go as you imagined it would—in fact, you can be sure it won't—but God the Initiator is also God the Finisher. He loves your son, your daughter, more than you could on your very best day.

There may be times when you find it necessary to allow your beloved child to live through tough consequences. After all, a child who drops out of school without a plan B is going to eventually have to support himself, even if that means slopping hogs for a living. Remember that, in the midst of these consequences, God still loves and pursues your child. Scripture reminds us that we may find ourselves or our kids as recipients of God's discipline and that God "disciplines those he loves" (Prov. 3:12). Sometimes the only way to get our attention is through pain.

What is the goal of the pain that comes from being disciplined? In Paul's letter to the Galatians, we see the endgame clearly: it is restoration. "Brothers and sisters, if someone is caught in a sin, you who live by the Spirit should restore that person gently" (Gal. 6:1). In the same way we as parents, on our good days, administer discipline to our children on their behalf, as God does it for us. The difference is that he controls all the circumstances of the creation and can design a restorative path that we would never dream of.

Remember the Vows!

If you have raised your kids in the church, you have likely had them either baptized or dedicated. In either case, two things happened that each of these public ceremonies have in common.

First, you as parents promised to raise your child in a home where following Jesus is a matter of practice, with the goal that your child would someday decide for herself to bow her knee to Christ as Lord. Second, the whole congregation was asked to promise their help in doing this. Two sets of vows: one from parents and one from the rest of the church.

I can't remember those vows quite as clearly as I do the ones I took the day of my wedding. But one can infer that, as when two people join in marriage, these promises are to bind both congregant and parent to our children (and all the children in our congregation) even when things are the hardest.

So what if one of those children commits a crime and is sent to prison for several years? On two occasions, young adults who were baptized as infants in Ted Martin's church committed crimes serious enough to draw multiyear sentences. The behavior of both kids drove their families to the end of their ropes and beyond. Both situations seemed hopeless.

Martin kept in touch with these men because he remembered the vow he and the congregation had made at the baptism of each: to help him grow up knowing and loving Jesus. The vow would not let Martin give up on these guys. When they had thoroughly burned their bridges with their parents, Ted stayed connected by visiting them in jail and having dinner and otherwise staying in touch when they were released.

Such stories don't always end happily. In fact, one of these fellows is back in church and the other isn't. But both are out of jail, holding jobs, and, in one case, raising a family. They have years of stable, crime-free life behind them now. Ted's rallying cry for himself and for us is "Remember the vows!"

The Story Is Not Over Yet

As I celebrated the birth of a grandson with a friend, he recalled a moment during his daughter, Eugenia's, sophomore year in college when she announced that she no longer could believe the Christian message. Eugenia is now happily married to a Christian man, has become a terrific elementary school teacher, and is deeply committed to her church, her city, and her faith.

When Eugenia made that announcement in college, it was hard for her parents to believe that the young woman's story was over.

They kept reminding themselves that a person's spiritual story is not over in that person's early twenties, thirties, forties, and beyond.

In our experience with our own kids or others who have hit rough patches, we would do well to remember that we see only what is past, what is present, and what is external. God alone knows about tomorrow, and God alone can see into the heart and mind of a man or woman.

We end this chapter where the prodigal story takes us. It is ultimately a story about the Father: his character, his longing, his love. This is the God who throws parties in heaven when he finally gets hold of that wandering soul, that man or woman who was in "a distant country" for years. He found you, and he can find your wayward child. Refuse to give up on your child. Encourage yourself with the knowledge that God hasn't.

Stories: Whether We Can See It or Not, God Is at Work in the Lives of Our Prodigal Children

George, a senior in college who had seemingly abandoned his faith, wrote the following to his father:

> From my perspective, I've been most alive in my faith during times when I am completely broken and surrendered to God. Sometimes I try to compromise things with God and say, "Here, you can have this part of my life, but I want to maintain control of this part." I know this isn't the attitude I need to have, but it is difficult for me to fully surrender *every* aspect of my life. Learning to let go of everything and give God total control will be a challenge for me, but I recognize that it is what I am called to do as a Christian. I think this is a big factor when it comes to my age group walking away from church in their college years. I don't like when things are outside my control, and I think you could say the same of many students . . .

Joan, now an adult with kids of her own, describes herself as "the one who walked away." Joan was the perfect church kid who

185

regularly read her Bible, attended every youth event, and seemed destined to follow God right through college. She didn't. For reasons unclear even now, Joan stopped following Jesus and lived life for many years apart from him. Her rift with God wasn't about partying, addiction, or joining a group of Satan worshipers. Joan just "walked away." Her Father and Shepherd went looking for her, found her, and brought her back.

Bob watched his daughter, Louisa, discard her faith in college just as he had discarded his during his college years. Louisa came to her senses as a young woman, just as Bob had as a young man. Someone Louisa had known for years was interested in dating her. The young man told her, however, "I don't want to go out with someone who isn't following Jesus." That was jarring enough to put Louisa on the path back home to her heavenly Father.

Then there is Josh's story. Josh was three years old when his parents' marriage broke up. For the next eight years Josh lived with his dad. Right about when he entered middle school and his dad was getting remarried, Josh moved in with his mom and his two sisters. In eighth grade Josh started getting into trouble. By the time he had moved in with his uncle a couple of years later, that trouble was escalating. He was doing drugs and ran away more than once. Then he and some buddies vandalized a used-car lot. As a result, he found himself in a juvenile residential program, one step short of jail.

Sometime during these years Josh also did a stint in drug rehab. It was at this low, low point that Josh's mom called her pastor, who asked her if Josh had been baptized (he had) and then reminded Josh's mom of God's promises toward his covenant children. "God cares about his children," the pastor said, and then added, "God is not out of reach."

Fast-forward twenty-five years. Josh is married and has two daughters, one who is head of her campus Christian fellowship and one who is studying to be a missionary. Their family is what Josh's sister has called "tight-knit." Josh and his wife, who had her own challenges and difficulties growing up, are Christians. Josh is not merely a churchgoer; he's a pillar and a role model. And he sounds to me like a world-class dad.

The worst may be happening right now, but remember Josh's story and take heart.

12

There's Hope for Your Great, Scary Expectations, Revisited

I remember driving from Pittsburgh to McLean, Virginia, to meet with a couple who gave a gift to the CCO every year. I thought they might be willing to give more if someone went and asked them. It was a great visit with a delightful couple, but here is the embarrassing part—I was too nervous to do the very thing I set out to do: ask for a bigger gift.

However, I did have plenty of time to think about my missed opportunity on the four-and-a-half-hour drive back.

I was chagrined enough to actually call the couple when I got home. "Ed, this is really embarrassing, but when I was with you I neglected to do the one thing that is most important to my job: to ask you for money."

He laughed. "Phyllis said after you left, 'Did he make the ask?' Don't worry, Dan, I made out the check as soon as you left."

An anxiety-laden fundraiser is sort of like a cowardly lion—he doesn't fit well in the job description.

If your child's growing independence or the oncoming college years have been a source of anxiety, I hope reading this book has helped alleviate some of your concerns. Like any parent, you will do a better job if you are less afraid.

You have seen evidence, based in Scripture, story, and research, that you and your spouse are still the two most influential people in the lives of your child. Hopefully, you have learned to let the data speak to your feelings, particularly when your adolescent is giving you those "get out of my life" signals.

In chapter 1, we began the book using the metaphor of a pathway (or pathways, plural) rather than a fix-it-all algorithm. Let's walk down that path one more time, noting the signposts along the way so we can continue to build our positive influence in the lives of our children. Let's pray for wisdom and take action. Go ahead and scribble some notes right here in the margins. Hey, it's my book and I give you permission. I'd love to read what you come up with, so if you have a moment, send what you've got to dipper@ccojubilee. org. (I'll get a real name for my email address when I grow up.)

The first juncture along the path (chap. 2) was clarifying what we are hoping for when we imagine our kids in their post-college adult lives. Here is the "success" definition I developed after reading through 310 responses on the topic: *The young adult Christian owns his or her faith in Jesus Christ, reflects it in priorities and decisions, and lives it in community with other believers, seeking to influence the watching world.* It is not so important that you like my definition but rather that you *have* a definition as a starting point. Otherwise, it is too easy to simply go with cultural notions of success. Jot your definition of spiritual success for your kids in the margin here.

The next marker on the path was in chapter 3, where we identified seven myths that threaten to undermine our efforts as Christian parents—remember those guys?

Myth 1: Parents are peripheral in the lives of emerging adults.

Myth 2: Christian professionals (not parents) have the primary responsibility for the spiritual nurture of emerging adults.

Myth 3: College is a time for emerging adults to sow their wild oats.

Myth 4: It is unrealistic to expect college students to attend church regularly.

Myth 5: Christian faith has no place in an intellectually rigorous environment such as college.

Myth 6: Saying it is enough.

Myth 7: "I've got a good kid!"

I've identified some of these myths through sociological research, some through parent focus groups, and some from anecdotes. Each is listed because it fits with what I hear and see from college students and their parents. The list is not intended to be exhaustive. As was the case with the success definition, you might have your own ideas, better suited to your experience as a parent.

Do you have any myths to add? Go ahead and jot them in the margin. Would you like to cross out some of mine because they don't resonate with you? In a minute, you can take your pen and whack away, but do a quick gut check first. Does the myth truly hold no power over you or do you just wish it didn't hold any power? Myths are sneaky like that. They like to stay undercover. But mark out any myth that doesn't work for you.

Be on guard for anything on the list. Keeping with the "path" metaphor, think of a myth as an item you can unwittingly carry in your backpack for miles and miles, eventually giving it to your kids so they can carry it on the next leg. It is not a good weight; it's just a heavy, useless one. So jot down one or two thoughts that might help you leave the myths behind.

As we move to the next stop on the path, the trail goes a bit uphill. You might remember chapter 4 on imperfect parents, where we got in touch with our foibles and failings.

Think for a moment: Where did you see yourself in that chapter? Maybe you didn't see yourself at all, because you are flawless (ha-ha!). You are a parent, for goodness' sake, so you have access to daily feedback on your shortcomings. So what are yours? Where do you feel most inadequate as a parent? Go ahead, write a couple of those imperfections in the margin.

Now pray for God to work in and through your weakness and watch what happens. Encourage yourself along the way by remembering how many screwups God has used in his history with the world to advance his kingdom. When you feel discouraged because of your imperfections, remember Abraham, Sarah, David, and Peter. God used the likes of them to build his kingdom. He will use you, imperfections and all, as he works in the life of your child. The whole business of God showing up in our weak places is real—and it is our only hope.

Moving to chapter 5, where we learned more about parental influence, the path turns downhill. You can breathe a little easier. Although as your child grows you no longer have control and the opportunity to issue directives as effectively, you still have influence. What were your thoughts about Stephen Covey's circles of influence and concern? About the concept of emotional bank accounts with your kids?

On the business of wielding influence, what did you decide to do more of or less of? Are you asking questions that invite conversation instead of giving orders? Can you more clearly prioritize and communicate clear expectations (just a few, not a bunch)? What specific actions can you take to build the reserves in your emotional bank account with your child?

Pull out the highlighter or keep using the pen, and mark one or two places where you want to build your influence. One or two actions.

I have never been privileged to follow a yellow brick road, but that is how I imagine the walk through chapter 6, because it is in faraway Oz that Dorothy learns that there is "no place like home." When it comes to helping our kids not only learn about but experience the gospel, there is no place like home.

With the help of Dan Allender and Brené Brown, we considered the benefit of giving our children age-appropriate glimpses into how God works in the hard places in our own lives—rather than presenting ourselves as finished products. We also talked about creating an environment where we identify and celebrate each kid's unique gifts rather than an environment that focuses on deficits.

How did you decide to better access the power available to you from under your own roof? More regular family dinners? That whole confessing and receiving forgiveness thing—how is that going? Don't give up on that one; just keep offending your family members, naming your offenses, and asking for their forgiveness. I'm serious about this. Even if you can't get anyone in your home to admit his or her wrongs, you can keep modeling healthy behavior. "Note to self: offend family members and apologize, asking specifically for forgiveness. Repeat."

Chapter 7 started with the surprising finding that adults—such as those in our congregations—are a big influence on our kids. We learned it takes a church to raise a child. Take time now to draw your relational map. Put yourself in the middle and arrange all the grown-ups you spend time with in a circle around your name. Draw lines to them like spokes on a wheel. Which of these would you like your child (and you) to be exposed to on a more regular basis? Who does not appear on the map who should? Among those adults whom you influence and who influence you, which have kids to whom your kids are connected? Maybe those kids can be drawn into their own circle around their own parents.

When the path brought us to chapter 8, we learned that kids who learn to "keep good company" in high school are prepared to do so in college. Try saying something like this to a younger child (going back to the mom who told her son he could no longer visit a friend who was a bad influence on him): "You know, Joey,

I was thinking the other day about the people in my life, particularly the other grown-ups. I decided to list all the people I spend time with and then put a smiley face by those who tend to make me a better person—more excited about God, or life, or both. Then I put a frowny face next to those who don't seem like a very good influence and who are mean or angry. If you were making a list like that, which people in your life would get the smiley face?"

Depending on the age and temperament, your child might just stare back at you in wonder and pity. Of course, you will have to adjust this conversation for age appropriateness. And don't lie. If you are not going to write down some adults' names with smileys or frownies, pluses or minuses, don't say you did. It'll be a good exercise for you too. We adults are hardly immune from good and bad peer influences.

The next stop along the path (chap. 9) was an encouragement regarding one of Christian parents' most consistent fears: the loss of faith during college. We learned more about navigating life inside and outside of the classroom. Remember Billy Riley's story? More than anything else, we learned what can happen when college students get plugged into Christian fellowship on campus and in the church.

When we stopped on the path at chapter 10, no one was more surprised than I. My research showed that individuals, young and old, learn more about God and become closer to him through adversity. As parents, we instinctively try to protect our kids from all suffering, hoping to hold off life's pain until they are grown up, launched, and on their way. Scripture and life experience suggests we are deluded. Kids, like adults, get closer to God when they have nowhere else to turn. Rather than seek to shield our kids from all suffering (which is impossible), we would do well to guide them into seeking God in the midst of struggles.

Make some notes in the margin here. Identify a time you suffered. Describe what God taught you through that suffering. Then fill in the blank in this sentence: "When I see my child suffering, I will remember to _____."

In chapter 11, we are nearly to the end of the path, but a good-sized stream is in the way. Your child is living with the consequences of a bad choice or a series of bad choices. It hurts you to watch, and you don't know exactly how to respond. Remember that, although the parable of the prodigal son is not a lesson on parenting, it is a lesson on God's character and his approach toward us when we move away from him. Examine your attitude and actions toward your child in light of this picture of God as Father. Remember also that God intends to finish the work he began with your child. The project may not be going as you expected—but God the Initiator is also God the Finisher. He loves your son, your daughter, more than you could on your very best day.

Write in the margin here, but keep it short and sweet. Focus on what is within your circle of influence and answer this question: What is one thing you are not going to do as a result of your child's choice(s) and what is one thing you are going to do?

With chapter 12, we come to the end of the path of this particular book. We have plenty of miles ahead, some of them beautiful and some very tough. God willing, you will have the privilege of continuing the journey with your kids and watching as they come to the path with sons, daughters, nieces, and nephews of their own. They will make the walk, all the while teaching the next hikers in your family what they have learned.

As you've traveled this path with me, did you notice the occasional breeze along the way or the sun breaking through the trees? That was a reminder that God walks every foot of every mile with us, whether on level ground with good footing or uphill over piles of rocks.

I now commend you to the care of our loving Lord Jesus Christ and invite you to do the same with your kids. Most of the good you so earnestly desire for the life of your child is well beyond your means to bring about. You don't have control, but you know someone who does. His name is Jesus, he of the easy yoke and the light burden (see Matt. 11:30). He is with you and with your child on this journey.

If you have just one arrow in your parenting quiver, make it the arrow of prayer. Come full circle to the beginning of this book where we acknowledged that God is the source of all wisdom. You know your own helplessness, and you probably sometimes forget that God's invitation to pray is itself expressed in parental terms: "Which of you, if your son asks for bread, will give him a stone?" (Matt. 7:9). We who imperfectly love our kids would do anything for them. God loves us with passion, purity, and power. Imagine how he loves to entertain our requests, particularly those on behalf of our own kids.

God is eager to walk this path with you. Keep bringing your kid(s) before the throne of God's grace.

As Ann Voskamp said, "Can God be counted on? Count blessings and find out how many of His bridges have already held."[1]

An Afterword for Fathers

What's the single biggest difference-maker in passing a vital Christian faith from one generation to the next?

It is fathers. In fact, I am writing this afterword as a bit of a stand-alone, because I know if you men are like me, you are not buying and reading many books on parenting.

In early 2014, a sociology professor at the University of Southern California published an unusual book. It is based on nearly forty years of research with 350 families, and it asks one question: Why do some families pass on faith from generation to generation while others do not?

The answers the sociologist (Vern Bengston) and his colleagues (Norella Putney and Susan Harris) found are, as you would expect from such a project, complicated.

Here is a part that isn't complicated: evangelical Christians who grow up with a warm, loving father to whom they are emotionally connected are 25 percent more likely to embrace Christian faith as adults.[1] A warm mom is important, but she makes a difference of just 1 percent.

Can you see why I am addressing this afterword to you? In all of my work, I've found no other cause that has anywhere near this kind of impact. Men, you have the chance to be a game changer for your son or daughter.

Here is a bit more of what Dr. Bengston has to say: "Fervent faith cannot compensate for a distant dad." Over and over in interviews, Professor Bengtson said, he found that "a father who is an exemplar, a pillar of the church, but doesn't provide warmth and affirmation to his kid does not have kids who follow him in his faith."[2]

There is an opportunity here, but if we are going to take advantage of it, we will need to unwind some perceptions and maybe change some of our own habits. Both statistically, and by our own experience, we who are part of the church see that women are generally more active in their faith and all of its parts than are men. I know it's true that many of us have benefited from a faithful mom or a praying grandmother. At home, which parent tends to form emotional bonds with the kids? It is the mom. As long as they provide well and are good moral examples, Christian dads who are disconnected from their kids might get a free pass. We men are known for being doers more than feelers, warriors who have to wrench a place for their families in a hostile world. Amen to the notion of "the warrior dad," but this is a warrior who deeply cares about his charges and is emotionally available to them.

I am talking about men who live life "all in," with what John Eldredge describes in *Wild at Heart* as a God-given desire for adventure. They don't have to look like a Roman gladiator or a Scottish warrior. One of the most adventuresome men I know is a kindly, soft-spoken gentleman who lives in Central America and works to help poor communities obtain small, potentially life-changing loans.

Men, you are not God, but next to him there is no one more influential in the life of your kids when it comes to following Jesus. Your wife can work her butt off to help your kids come to know the Lord Christ, but she can't take your place. You can yourself be a shining example at your church, but if you have no ongoing bond with your kids, the whole project may very well go up in flames.

Make it your highest priority in life from here on out to have a warm, open relationship with each of your children. Remember that every son will "crawl over broken glass for his father's approval" and that every daughter will learn whether she is worthy and beautiful from you more than anyone else. Your kids need so desperately what only you can give them.

Acknowledgments

This project never would have achieved lift-off without the guidance and editorial feedback of my book coach, Bonnie Budzowski. Derek Melleby, Don Opitz, and Walt Mueller gave timely encouragement and good counsel early on. Thanks to Rick Stauffer, Adam Jackely, Chris Thompson, Chris Buda, Bill and Angie Glaze, Dave DiDinato, and Ted Martin for organizing focus groups. Thanks too to those who participated in the groups and the 310 others who helped with the "success definition."

I'd also like to acknowledge the CCO's leadership: our excellent board of directors, along with our executive and leadership teams. You gave both encouragement and permission at just the right times. Thanks to my two assistants, Beverly Cwalina and Gail Jones, who proofread, formatted, and generally got neck-deep into this project. Special thanks to archivist/librarian Lucy Jones who answered the "I need help with citations" alarm and gave away part of her life to help.

Deen and Margaret, thanks for your home! Paul, Ric, Jonathan, and Todd, thanks for helping me live into what I believe. For every person who allowed me to tell his or her story, bless you!

Carol, Jack, Spence, Eliza, and Annie, you continue to make this family journey, with all its ups and downs, a joy.

If you like the book, credit these fine people, but if you don't, let them off the hook. I know I am forgetting someone, and that is grievous to me. Think of the great reward that awaits in heaven!

Notes

Chapter 1: A Foundation of Wisdom

1. See Christian Smith and Patricia Snell, *Souls in Transition: The Religious and Spiritual Lives of Emerging Adults* (Oxford: Oxford University Press, 2009).

2. My thinking in this section has been influenced by the writings of Tremper Longman III, particularly his book *How to Read Proverbs* (Downers Grove, IL: InterVarsity Press, 2002).

Chapter 3: Seven Myths That Might Be Sabotaging Your Parenting

1. Christian Smith and Patricia Snell, *Souls in Transition: The Religious and Spiritual Lives of Emerging Adults* (Oxford: Oxford University Press, 2009), 222, 226, 229.

2. Ibid., 284.

3. Ibid.

4. Ibid.

5. "Six Reasons Young People Leave Church," The Barna Group, September 28, 2011, https://www.barna.org/teens-next-gen-articles/528-six-reasons-young -christians-leave-church. Accessed October 7, 2015.

6. See Mark A. Noll, *The Scandal of the Evangelical Mind* (Grand Rapids: Eerdmans, 1994).

7. Brené Brown, *The Gifts of Imperfect Parenting: Raising Children with Courage, Compassion, and Connection*, audiobook (Louisville, CO: Sounds True, 2013).

Chapter 4: You Are Nowhere Close to Being a Perfect Parent

1. Laura F. Deutsch, "Did I Do Enough?" *Pittsburgh Post-Gazette*, February 8, 2014.

2. David Kinnaman and Gabe Lyons, *Unchristian: What a New Generation Really Thinks about Christianity . . . And Why It Matters* (Grand Rapids: Baker, 2007), 29–30.

Chapter 5: Losing Control as Your Kid Grows

1. Smith and Snell, *Souls in Transition*, 222, 226, 229.
2. Ibid., 284.
3. Ibid.
4. Ibid.
5. Key Concepts: "Executive Function," Center on the Developing Child, Harvard University, http://developingchild.harvard.edu/key_concepts/executive_function/.
6. Michael G. Conner, "Crisis Intervention for Teenagers—A Family Guide," Bend Psychological Services, http://www.crisiscounseling.org/CrisisIntervention Teens.htm.
7. Stephen R. Covey, *The 7 Habits of Highly Effective People: Powerful Lessons in Personal Change* (New York: Simon & Schuster, 2013), 83.
8. Smith and Snell, *Souls in Transition*, 284.
9. Covey, *The 7 Habits of Highly Effective People*, 92.
10. The Family Dinner Project, http://thefamilydinnerproject.org.

Chapter 6: Center on Home

1. Ben Carson and Cecil Murphy, *Gifted Hands: The Ben Carson Story* (Grand Rapids: Zondervan, 2011), 45.
2. Brené Brown, *The Gifts of Imperfect Parenting: Raising Children with Courage, Compassion, and Connection* (Louisville, CO: Sounds True, 2013).
3. Dan B. Allender, *How Children Raise Parents: The Art of Listening to Your Family* (Colorado Springs: WaterBrook Press, 2005), 2.
4. Attributed to D. T. Niles.
5. Tom Rath, *StrengthsFinder 2.0* (Washington, DC: Gallup Press, 2007), i.
6. Ibid.
7. "CCO recognized as Best Christian Place to Work," Coalition for Christian Outreach, May 1, 2015, http://ccojubilee.org/news/cco-recognized-as-best-christian-place-to-work/16/.
8. Angela Thomas with Amy Simpson, "Hope for Single Parents," *Today's Christian Woman*, September 2013.

Chapter 7: Invite Community

1. "Don't Trust Anyone over 30, Unless It's Jack Weinberg," *Berkeley Daily Planet*, April 6, 2000, http://www.berkeleydailyplanet.com/issue/2000-04-06/article /759.
2. Kenda Creasy Dean, *Almost Christian: What the Faith of Our Teenagers Is Telling the American Church* (New York: Oxford University Press, 2010), 45–60.
3. Ibid., 52.

Chapter 8: Invite Kids

1. M. K. Smith, "Robert Putnam," in the encyclopedia of informal education (infed.org, 2012).

Chapter 10: When the Wheels Are Falling Off

1. John Fischer, *12 Steps for the Recovering Pharisee (Like Me)* (Bloomington, MN: Bethany House, 2000).

Chapter 11: The Worst Is Happening

1. What Churchill actually said was, "Never give in, never give in, never, never, never—in nothing great or small, large or petty—never give in except to convictions of honour and good sense." See "Quotes FAQ," The Churchill Centre, 2015, http ://www.winstonchurchill.org/resources/quotations/quotes-faq.

2. Amy Ziettlow, "Religion Runs in the Family," interview with Vern Bengston, *Christianity Today*, September 20, 2013, http://www.christianitytoday.com/ct /2013/august-web-only/religion-runs-in-family.html?start=3.

Chapter 12: There's Hope for Your Great, Scary Expectations, Revisited

1. Ann Voskamp, *One Thousand Gifts: A Dare to Live Fully Right Where You Are* (Grand Rapids: Zondervan, 2012).

An Afterword for Fathers

1. Vern L. Bengston, *Families and Faith: How Religion Is Passed Down Across Generations* (New York: Oxford University Press, 2014), 78.

2. Mark Oppenheimer, "Book Explores Ways Faith Is Kept, or Lost, over Generations," *New York Times*, January 31, 2014, http://www.nytimes.com/2014 /02/01/us/book-explores-ways-faith-is-kept-or-lost-over-generations.html?_r=1.

CCO

transforming college students

to transform the world

THE COALITION FOR CHRISTIAN OUTREACH
CALLS COLLEGE STUDENTS TO SERVE JESUS CHRIST

WITH THEIR ENTIRE LIVES.

CCO MINISTRY IS DISTINCT IN THREE WAYS:

We develop students to be passionate leaders
who serve Jesus Christ in their studies, jobs, communities,
and families.

We serve together with the church,
inviting students into the lives of local congregations.

We design each ministry to fit the needs of every
campus we serve.

FIND OUT MORE: **ccojubilee.org**

Dan Dupee is chairman of the board of the Coalition for Christian Outreach, a Pittsburgh-based campus ministry working annually with over 32,000 students on over 115 campuses. He brings together biblical truth, sociological research, college transition findings, and focus group work with parents of adolescents to develop principles that are fresh, clarifying additions to a growing body of research on teen faith development. Dan and his wife, Carol, are the parents of four children. They live in the northern suburbs of Pittsburgh, Pennsylvania.